CUC

366 readings from
BUDDHISM

Also in the Global Spirit Library

366 readings from Islam

366 readings from Christianity

366 readings from Taoism and Confucianism

366 readings from Hinduism

366 readings from Judaism

THE GLOBAL SPIRIT LIBRARY

366 readings from

BUDDHISM

edited by

ROBERT VAN DE WEYER

THE PILGRIM PRESS
CLEVELAND, OHIO

ARTHUR JAMES
NEW ALRESFORD, UK

First published in USA and Canada by
The Pilgrim Press,
700 Prospect Avenue East, Cleveland, Ohio 44115

First published in English outside North America by
Arthur James Ltd,
46a West Street, New Alresford, UK, SO24 9AU

05 04 03 02 01 00   5 4 3 2 1

North America ISBN 0-8298-1385-3
English language outside North America ISBN 0 85305 453 3

Typeset in Monotype Joanna by
Strathmore Publishing Services, London N7

Printed by
Tien Wah Press, Singapore

CONTENTS

SERIES INTRODUCTION

The Global Spirit Library is the first comprehensive collection of the spiritual literature of the world, presented in accessible form. It is aimed at people who belong to a particular religious community, and wish to broaden their spiritual outlook; and at the much larger group, perhaps the majority of people in the world today, who have little or no attachment to a religious community, but seek spiritual wisdom. Each book contains the major writings of one of the world's spiritual traditions.

Much of the world's spiritual literature was designed to be read or heard in small portions, allowing ample time for personal reflection. Following this custom, the books in *The Global Spirit Library* each consist of an annual cycle of daily readings. Two or more books may be read in parallel at different times of the day; or an entire book may be read straight through. Again following a time-honoured practice, many of the original texts have been condensed.

Spiritual traditions differ from one another in their theological formulations; and the history of humankind is blighted by rivalry between different religious communities. Yet theology is no more than human speculation about truths that are beyond the grasp of the human mind. The writings in these books amply demonstrate that, as men and women actually experience these truths within themselves and others, divisions and rivalries fade, and unity is found. May the third millennium be an era of spiritual unity across the globe.

INTRODUCTION

Buddha means 'enlightened person'. A Buddhist is someone who follows the teachings of a particular enlightened person, called Gautama.

In approximately the year 534 BCE, in northern India, Gautama attained enlightenment, while sitting cross-legged under a tree. He then devoted the rest of his life to teaching others the spiritual wisdom he had acquired. He established a large Community of monks and nuns, and also had numerous lay disciples. Although commonly referred to as the Buddha, he saw himself as one of countless enlightened teachers, who appear in every age and in every society. In the centuries after his death Buddhism spread thoughout southern and eastern Asia.

THE TEACHINGS OF THE BUDDHA

Soon after the Buddha had died, the monks of his Community began the task of recording his teachings. These records were made in Pali, a literary variant of the language which the Buddha himself spoke. The Pali Canon, as the records are known, is immensely long, running into many volumes, and is highly repetitive, with similar passages often appearing in several places. Yet certain parts manifestly contain the essence of his teachings; while other parts have come to be regarded as developing his teachings with special beauty and clarity.

The Pali Canon is not in any way a biography of the Buddha; and the Buddha discouraged any attention to his own particular circumstances and personality. The place where a sermon was delivered, is usually given, as are the names of people he encountered. Thus we know that his ministry was largely confined to the kingdoms of Magadha in northern India, and Kossala, which corresponds roughly with modern Nepal; and he mixed freely with people of all social classes. Nonetheless the Pali Canon contains a vivid account of the period immediately after his enlightenment; and in one sermon he gives a glimpse of his early life. Later biographies, which suggest that he grew up as a prince, are speculative.

The origin of suffering

The Buddha attained enlightenment sitting under a tree on the bank of the river Nerengara at Uruvela. He remained there, sitting cross-legged, for seven days without interruption, enjoying the bliss of salvation.

Then during the first part of the night he meditated on the chain of causation:

From ignorance spring body, speech and mind.

From body, speech and mind springs consciousness.

From consciousness spring the names and forms of
   objects.

From the names and forms spring the six senses of
   seeing, hearing, smelling, tasting, touching and
   thinking.

From the six senses springs contact with objects.

From contact springs sensation.

From sensation springs desire.

From desire springs attachment.

From attachment springs birth.

From birth spring old age, death, grief, pain and
   despair.

In this manner the whole mass of suffering in the world originates.

Mahavagga I: I. I—2

The destruction of suffering

The Buddha continued to meditate on the chain of causation.

By the destruction of ignorance, body, speech and
mind are destroyed.

By the destruction of body, speech and mind, consciousness is destroyed.

By the destruction of consciousness, the names and
forms of objects are destroyed.

By the destruction of the names and forms of objects,
the six senses are destroyed.

By the destruction of the six senses, contact is
destroyed.

By the destruction of contact, sensation is destroyed.

By the destruction of sensation, desire is destroyed.

By the destruction of desire, attachment is destroyed.

By the destruction of attachment, birth is destroyed.

By the destruction of birth, old age, death, grief, pain
and despair are destroyed.

In this manner the whole mass of suffering in the world
may cease.

When the Buddha had finished meditating on the chain
of causation, his uncertainties faded, and he understood the
nature of all things.

Mahavagga 1:1.2—3

The first lay disciples

At the end of seven days the Buddha emerged from a state of meditation, rose up, and went to a banyan tree. He sat cross-legged for a further seven days without interruption, enjoying the bliss of salvation.

A priest, with an arrogant disposition, came and sat near the Buddha. Then he asked the Buddha: 'What are the characteristics of true priests?' The Buddha replied: 'True priests are those who have abandoned all sins, who are free from arrogance, who are pure and self-controlled, who are wise and learned, who have achieved a high degree of holiness, and whose behaviour does no harm to any living being.'

At the end of seven days the Buddha emerged from a state of meditation, rose up, and went to tree known as Raga-yatana. He sat cross-legged for a further seven days without interruption, enjoying the bliss of salvation.

Two merchants, Tapussa and Bhallika, passed by. They felt prompted to pay homage to the Buddha, offering him rice-cakes and honey. The Buddha wondered whether it was appropriate for him, having attained enlightenment, to accept their gift. But after a while he felt prompted to do so; and he ate the rice-cakes and the honey. Then Tapussa and Bhallika said: 'We put our trust in you, enlightened one, and in the Way which you have followed. We ask you to accept us as your disciples, from today until the end of our lives.' Thus these two merchants were the first lay disciples of the Buddha.

Mahavagga I:2. 1–3; 4. 1–5

The decision to preach

At the end of seven days the Buddha emerged from a state of meditation, rose up, and returned to the banyan tree.

When he had sat down, he thought: 'I have apprehended spiritual truth, which is profound and hard to grasp. It brings serenity to the mind, and cannot be known through reason; it is intelligible only to the wise. Most people, however, are concerned only to satisfy their desires; and so they are bound by the chain of causation. Therefore, if I preach spiritual truth, they will not understand my words; so the only consequence of preaching is that I shall become weary and cross.'

Then the Buddha was filled with compassion. In his mind's eye he looked across the world. He saw some people whose souls were covered with only a few specks of dust; and some whose souls were darkened by a thick layer of dust; some people who were good, and some who were evil; some people who were easy to instruct, and some who were difficult. He thought: 'Let those whose souls are open to receive the truth, hear the truth. The Way, which I have followed, is joyful and fine.'

Mahavagga 1:5.1–2, 10, 12

The five monks in Isipatana

The Buddha now asked himself: 'To whom shall I preach first? Who will understand easily what I have to say?' He thought of five monks, who had served him while he was striving to attain enlightenment. He remembered that they lived at the deer-park in Isipatana; so he set off to that city.

On the road he met a monk whose sect required him to be naked. The naked monk said: 'Friend, your expression is serene, and your complexion is pure and bright. Whose teachings do you follow?' The Buddha replied: 'I have myself apprehended the truth; I do not need a teacher. In order to found a kingdom of truth, I am going to the city of Isipatana.' The naked monk shook his head, and went away.

When the five monks saw the Buddha in the distance, they said to one another: 'He has given up striving for enlightenment, and has returned to a life of comfort. We shall not greet him, nor shall we rise up as he approaches; we shall merely invite him to sit beside us, if he chooses.' But as he drew closer, they found themselves rising up, and going forward to greet him. One of them fetched a bowl of water to wash his feet. One by one they welcomed him, calling him 'Friend'.

He said to them: 'No longer call me "Friend". I have won immortality. I shall teach you the spiritual truth which I have learnt. If you follow the Way which I shall show you, you will also understand the truth; you will encounter the truth face to face.' The five monks said: 'You have never spoken in this manner before.'

Mahavagga 1:6.1, 5–12, 16

The eightfold path

The five monks agreed to listen to what the Buddha had to say. So the Buddha preached to them: 'There are two extremes which should be avoided. The first extreme is a life devoted to pleasure; this is degrading and worthless. The second extreme is a life devoted to self-mortification; this is painful and worthless. The middle path, between these two extremes, leads to insight, which leads to wisdom, which leads to serenity, which leads to truth, which leads to nirvana.

'The middle path is actually the eightfold path. This is: right vision, right purpose, right speech, right action, right livelihood, right effort, right awareness, and right concentration.'

Mahavagga 1:6.17–18

The four noble truths

'There are four noble truths. The first noble truth is suffering. Birth is suffering; decay is suffering; illness is suffering; and death is suffering. The presence of objects we hate, is suffering; separation from objects we love, is suffering; not obtaining what we desire, is suffering. In short, every form of attachment is suffering.

'The second noble truth is the cause of suffering. Desire for pleasure, desire for existence, and desire for wealth, cause suffering.

'The third noble truth is the cessation of suffering. The cessation of desire, which consists in the absence of all attachment, leads to the cessation of suffering.

'The fourth noble truth is the path that leads to the cessation of suffering. This is the eightfold path of right vision, right purpose, right speech, right action, right livelihood, right effort, right awareness, and right concentration.'

Mahavagga 1:6.19–22

The first monastic disciples

The Buddha concluded: 'So long as I did not understand these four noble truths, I could not realize perfect wisdom; but when I understood these four noble truths, I realized perfect wisdom. I have been saved from the cycle of birth and death; I shall not be born again!'

The five monks were delighted at the Buddha's teaching. One of them, called Kondanna, understood it fully, and declared: 'That which begins, also ends.' The Buddha exclaimed: 'Kondanna has perceived the truth!' And he changed his name to Annatakondanna.

Then Annatakondanna said to the Buddha: 'Please receive me as a disciple, and ordain me as a monk of your Community.' The Buddha agreed to this request, saying: 'You will lead a holy life, for the sake of extinguishing all suffering.'

The Buddha continued to instruct the other four monks on the Way. After a while two of them, Vappa and Bhadiya, also understood his teaching fully, and declared: 'That which begins, also ends.' They too asked for ordination. The Buddha agreed, saying: 'Lead a holy life, in order to extinguish all suffering.'

The Buddha continued to instruct the remaining two monks, Mahanama and Assagi, on the Way. Eventually they also understood his teaching fully, and declared: 'That which begins, also ends.' The Buddha agreed to ordain them.

Mahavagga 1:6.29, 32—37

Freedom from attachment

The Buddha said to the five monks: 'The body is not the soul.
If the body were the soul, it would not be subject to disease.
Sensation is not the soul. Perception is not the soul. Thought
is not the soul. Consciousness is not the soul. None of these
is the soul, because they are perishable; and that which is
perishable causes suffering.

'Those who understand the truth, become weary of the
body, weary of sensation, weary of perception, weary of
thought, and weary of consciousness. In their weariness they
divest themselves of all attachment; and without attachment
they are free. When they are free, they become aware of their
freedom. Then they realize that they will never be reborn;
their holiness is complete; never again will they return to this
world.'

The five monks were delighted at the Buddha's words.
And having understood his words, they became free from all
attachment to the world. Thus they were released from sensuality, desire, illusion, and ignorance.

Mahavagga 1:6.38–43, 46–47

The rich young man

Living in Isipatana was a rich young man, called Yasa. He had three mansions, one for winter, one for summer, and one for the rainy season. One evening, while he was at his mansion for the rainy season, he fell asleep earlier than usual. In due course the female musicians, who had been playing for him, also fell asleep.

Yasa awoke at dawn, and looked at the musicians sleeping nearby. One had her lute leaning against her armpit; another had her tabor leaning against her neck; another had dishevelled hair; another had saliva dripping from her mouth; and all of them were muttering in their sleep. It seemed to him that he was in a spiritual cemetery; and he felt utterly weary of worldly pleasures.

He put on gilt shoes, left his mansion, and went to the deer-park where the Buddha was staying. Yasa exclaimed to the Buddha: 'In my life there is great suffering and great danger.' The Buddha replied: 'Here there is neither suffering nor danger. Come and sit down, and I shall teach you the Way.'

The Buddha could see that Yasa was ready to understand the four noble truths; he was like a spotless white cloth, ready to take dye. So when the Buddha had finished explaining them, Yasa declared: 'That which begins, also ends.'

Mahavagga 1:7. 1–4, 6

The first female disciples

In the meantime Yasa's mother had been to the mansion; and finding that Yasa was missing, she rushed to tell her husband, Yasa's father. Yasa's father sent servants on horseback in every direction to search for Yasa; and he himself went to the deer-park.

When Yasa's father arrived at the deer-park, the Buddha assured him that he would soon see his son. The Buddha then taught Yasa's father the Way. When the Buddha had finished, Yasa's father said: 'You overturn all conventional knowledge; you have revealed what is hidden; you are a lamp in the darkness. I commit myself to the Way; and I ask you to accept me as your disciple, from today until the end of my life.'

Then Yasa's father saw his son a little distance away, in a state of deep meditation. He said to his son: 'Your mother is beside herself with anxiety at your disappearance; go and re-assure her that you are safe.' The Buddha said to Yasa's father: 'Is it right that Yasa should return to the world, and enjoy its pleasures as he did before?' Yasa's father replied: 'No, it is not. I am glad that he is now free from all attachment to worldly things. Will you, Lord, consent to take a meal at my house, with Yasa waiting on you.' The Buddha agreed.

Yasa now asked to be ordained as a monk in the Buddha's Community; and the Buddha immediately ordained him. Then they set out to the house of Yasa's father. At the meal Yasa's mother and wife sat near the Buddha, and he taught them the Way. They became his first female disciples.

Mahavagga 1:7.7, 9–15; 8.1, 3

More disciples

Four other rich young men, who were friends of Yasa, heard that he had become a monk, shaving off his hair and beard, and putting on yellow robes. And they said to one another: 'The spiritual teaching which has induced him to do this, must be most unusual.' They went to see Yasa, and he took them to see the Buddha.

The Buddha spoke to them about the four noble truths. When he had finished, they too asked to be received as his disciples, and ordained as monks. He agreed to their request, saying: 'Lead a holy life, in order to extinguish all suffering.' He continued to teach them, and they became free from all attachments. There were now eleven monks in the Buddha's Community.

A further fifty young men, who were friends of these new monks, came to see them; and they took them to see the Buddha. When they had heard his teaching, they too asked to be ordained as monks. So now there were sixty-one monks in the Buddha's Community.

Mahavagga 1:9. 1–4; 10. 1–4

Commission to preach

The Buddha now said to his monks: 'Go out in a spirit of compassion, and take to others the benefits which you have received. Teach the Way, which is glorious at the beginning, in the middle, and at the end. Urge people to lead lives of perfect holiness. There are many people whose souls are covered by only a few specks of dust. If the Way is not preached to them, they cannot be saved; but if they hear about the Way, they will follow it.'

As a result of their preaching the monks brought people from many regions and countries, who wished to be received as disciples and ordained as monks. The monks became weary from constantly travelling to and from the Buddha. The Buddha reflected on this matter in solitude. Then he gave the

monks permission to receive and ordain people themselves. He added: 'Before being ordained as monks, people should raise their arms, join their hands together, and declare three times their commitment to the Way and to the Community.'

Mahavagga 1: 11. 1;
12. 1–4

The young men and the prostitute

The Buddha decided to go to Uruvela. In the course of the journey he left the road, and sat down at the foot of a tree. Nearby a party of thirty young men were playing. One of the young men had brought a prostitute; and while the men were engaged in some game, she grabbed their belongings, and ran away.

When the young men realized what had happened, they went in search of her. They found the Buddha sitting under a tree, told him what had happened, and asked if he had seen the woman. The Buddha said: 'Let me ask you a question. Which is better for you: to search for a woman; or to search for yourselves?' The young men replied: 'It would be better for us to search for ourselves.' So the Buddha invited them to sit beside him, and he taught them the Way.

When he had finished speaking, they declared: 'That which begins, also ends.' Then they asked the Buddha to receive them as his disciples, and to ordain them as monks in his Community.' He consented to their request.

Mahavagga 1:14.1−5

The fire sermon

Having stayed at Uruvela for some time, the Buddha decided to go to a mountain near Gaya. He was accompanied by a thousand monks.

When they arrived, he addressed the monks: 'Everything is burning. How is everything burning? The eye is burning. The ear is burning. The nose is burning. The tongue is burning. The body is burning. Thought is burning. The mental impressions, made by what the senses perceive, are burning. And the sensations produced by these mental impressions, whether they are pleasant or painful, are burning.

'With what fires are they burning? They are burning with the fire of desire, the fire of anger, and the fire of ignorance. They are burning with the fire of anxiety about birth, decay and death. They are burning with the fires of suffering and despair.

'Those who follow the Way, become weary of the senses. They become weary of the mental impressions made by what the senses perceive. They become weary of the sensations produced by these mental impressions, whether they are pleasant or painful. In their weariness of all these, they divest themselves of all attachment; and without attachment they are free. When they are free, they become aware of their freedom. Then they realize that they will never be reborn; their holiness is complete; never again will they return to this world.'

When they had heard these words, all the thousand monks became free of attachment to the world.

Mahavagga 1:21.1–4

The king's five wishes

The Buddha now led the monks to Rajagaha, where they stayed in the bamboo garden. The king, called Bimbisara, heard that the Buddha had arrived, and went to see him. He bowed down to the Buddha, and then sat down near him. The Buddha explained to the king the four noble truths. The king understood fully all that the Buddha said, and exclaimed: 'That which begins, also ends.'

The king then said: 'When I was a young prince, I had five wishes; and these are now fulfilled. My first wish was to be crowned as king. My second wish was that an enlightened teacher would enter my kingdom. My third wish was that I might pay my respects to this teacher. My fourth wish was that this teacher might teach me. And my fifth wish was that I might understand what he taught.' The king then invited the Buddha and his monks to eat with him the following day.

At the meal the king served the Buddha and his monks with his own hands. After the meal the king sat next to the Buddha, and the Buddha spoke to him about spiritual matters.

Mahavagga 1:22.1–3, 7–11, 15, 18

A summary of the Way

At that time another spiritual leader, called Sangaya, was staying in Rajagaha, with a community of two hundred and fifty
monks. Amongst these monks were two young men, called
Sariputta and Moggallana; and they had agreed that, if one of
them attained nirvana, he would show the other how to attain it.

One day Sariputta saw Assagi, one of the Buddha's first
monks, in the centre of Rajagaha, begging for food. When
Assagi had finished, and was returning to the bamboo garden,
Sariputta approached him, and said: 'Friend, your expression
is serene, and your complexion is pure and bright. Who is
your teacher, and what are his teachings?' Assagi replied: 'My
teacher is the Buddha; and I follow his teachings.'

Sariputta persisted: 'What are his teachings?' Assagi replied: 'I am only a young disciple, friend; and I have only
recently adopted his teachings. So I cannot explain them in
detail.' Sariputta said: 'Tell me as much or as little as you like.
I want the spirit of his teachings; I am not concerned with
the letter.' Assagi said: 'The Buddha explains that all objects
have a cause; and since they have a cause, they also cease.
That is the spirit of his teaching.'

Sariputta understood this teaching fully, and declared:
'That which begins, also ends.' Then he added: 'This is the
Way by which all suffering ceases, and nirvana is attained.'

Mahavagga 1:23. 1–5

A community's conversion

Sariputta went at once to Moggallana, and told him that he had found the means of attaining nirvana. Moggallana replied: 'Let us go the Buddha who teaches this, and become his disciples.' Sariputta said: 'Let us first go and speak to the other disciples of our present teacher.'

So they went and told the other disciples of Sangaya about the Buddha. The other disciples replied: 'We have great respect for your judgement. If you become disciples of the Buddha, so shall we.'

Sariputta and Moggallana then went to Sangaya himself, and told him that they intended to become disciples of the Buddha. Sangaya replied: 'Do not go to the Buddha. Let all three of us share the leadership of this community.' Sariputta and Moggallana insisted that they intended to go to the Buddha; and Sangaya repeated his offer. Sariputta insisted for a third time, and again Sangaya repeated his offer. So Sariputta and Moggallana left, taking with them the whole of Sangaya's community. Sangaya vomited.

When the Buddha saw them coming, he declared: 'Sariputta and Moggallana will be most worthy disciples.' The two men went up to the Buddha, prostrated themselves, and asked if he would receive themselves and their companions as his disciples, and ordain them as monks in his Community. The Buddha agreed, saying: 'Lead holy lives, in order to extinguish all suffering.'

Mahavagga 1:24. 1–4

Anger against the Buddha

By this time many distinguished young men had become
monks in the Buddha's Community. This caused anger, and
people said to one another: 'Gautama causes men not to become fathers, and thus makes families extinct. He has ordained as monks many of the finest noblemen in the land.
Already the entire community of Sangaya has gone over to
him. Who will be the next to be led by him?'

The Buddha's monks heard that people were becoming
angry, and they reported it to the Buddha. The Buddha
replied: 'This anger will not last long; after seven days it will
be over. If they revile you, say this to them: that those who
follow true teaching, are true heroes. And ask them by what
means I lead people, except by the power of the truth.'

During the following days the Buddha's monks were
frequently reviled. And they replied: 'Those who follow true
teaching, are true heroes. By what means do you think the
Buddha leads people, except by the power of the truth?' The
people understood these words; and within seven days their
anger against the Buddha had subsided.

Mahavagga 1:24.5–7

Awareness of breathing

The Buddha was staying amongst the Kurus. He addressed his monks: 'There is only one way to purify yourselves, to transcend sorrow and grief, to extinguish suffering and misery, to live serenely, and to realize nirvana: this is through applying the four forms of awareness.

'The first is awareness of the body. You may go into the forest, and sit at the foot of a tree; or you may go into an empty room. You cross your legs, and hold your body erect. You observe yourself as you inhale, and observe yourself as you exhale. Inhaling a long breath, you are aware that a long breath has been inhaled. Exhaling a long breath, you are aware that you are exhaling a long breath. You are equally aware of inhaling and exhaling a short breath. You reflect: "Aware of my whole body, I shall inhale." And then you reflect: "Aware of my whole body, I shall exhale." Then you reflect: "Calming my bodily forces, I shall inhale." And then you reflect: "Calming my bodily forces, I shall exhale."

'As you become aware of the body in this manner, you understand that the body continually comes into being and passes away. This understanding concentrates the mind, and enables the mind to become self-sufficient, not grasping at external objects.'

Maha Satipatthana Sutta 1–2

Awareness of actions and elements

'When you are walking, you are aware that you are walking. You reflect: "I am walking." When you are standing, or sitting, or lying down, you are aware of your posture. In whatever way you hold your body, you are aware of it. As you observe the body in this manner, you understand that the body continually grows and continually decays. This understanding concentrates the mind, and enables the mind to become self-sufficient, not grasping at external objects.

'Similarly, when you are going out or returning, when you are looking at something or looking away from it, when you are drawing in your limbs or stretching them out, and when you are eating or drinking, you are aware of what you are doing.

'As you observe the body, from the soles of the feet to the crown of the head, you understand the body as something enclosed in skin, and full of various organs and substances. It is like a bag, tied at both ends, which has been filled with various kinds of grain.

'As you observe the body, whatever it is doing and in whatever posture it is held, you understand that, like any other living being, it is composed of the four elements of earth, water, heat and air.

'If you were to see a dead body lying in a field, you would reflect that it was composed of the same elements as your own body; and that your body will soon suffer the same fate.'

Maha Satipatthana Sutta 3–7

Awareness of sensations and thoughts

'The second form of awareness is awareness of sensations. When you have a pleasurable sensation, you are aware of it, reflecting: "I am having a pleasurable sensation." When you have a painful sensation, you are aware of it, reflecting: "I am having a painful sensation." When you are having a neutral sensation, you are aware of it, reflecting: "I am having a neutral sensation." You are also aware of whether the sensation is associated with something material, or something spiritual. As you observe sensations in this manner, you understand that sensations continually come into being and pass away. This understanding concentrates the mind, and enables the mind to become self-sufficient, not grasping at external objects.

'The third form of awareness is awareness of thoughts. You are aware when your thoughts are filled with desire; and you are aware when your thoughts are empty of desire. You are aware when your thoughts are filled with hate; and you are aware when your thoughts are empty of hate. You are aware when your thoughts are deluded, and when they are free of delusion. You are aware when your thoughts are attentive and inattentive, elevated and not elevated, high and low, still and wandering, free and constrained. In each case you reflect: "My thoughts are filled with desire." And so on. As you observe thoughts in this manner, you understand that thoughts continually come into being and pass away. This understanding concentrates the mind, and enables the mind to become self-sufficient, not grasping at external objects.'

Maha Satipatthana Sutta 11—12

Awareness of mental states

'The fourth form of awareness is awareness of mental states. You observe mental objects in the context of the five hindrances.

'The first hindrance is sensual desire. When you have a sensuous desire, you reflect: "I have a sensuous desire." When you do not have a sensuous desire, you are aware of this also.

'The second hindrance is malice. When you have malice, you reflect: "I have malice." When you do not have malice, you are aware of this also.

'The third hindrance is inertia. When your mind is inert, you reflect: "I am mentally inert." When you are not inert, you are aware of this also.

'The fourth hindrance is distraction. When your mind is distracted, you reflect: "I am distracted." When you are not distracted, you are aware of this also.

'The fifth hindrance is doubt. When you are troubled by doubts, you reflect: "I am troubled by doubts." When you are not troubled by doubts, you are aware of this also.

'As you observe hindrances in this manner, you understand that hindrances continually come into being and pass away. This understanding concentrates the mind, and enables the mind to become self-sufficient, not grasping at external objects.'

Maha Satipatthana Sutta 13

Awareness of existence, mind and enlightenment

'By observing mental states, you become aware of the five means of clinging to existence. These are the body; sensations; perceptions; concepts; and consciousness. As you observe the five means of clinging to existence, you understand that they continually come into being and pass away.

'By observing mental states, you also become aware of the twelve bases of mental activity. These include the faculties sight, hearing, smell, taste, touch, and thought. They also include consciousness of these faculties, of the objects which they perceive, and of the relationship between the faculties and the objects perceived by them. And they include consciousness of these faculties being dormant, of not perceiving any objects, and of there being no relationship between the faculties and external objects.

'By observing mental states, you also become aware of the seven factors of enlightenment. These are awareness of awareness, investigation of the Way, vigour, joy, serenity, concentration and equanimity. When any of these factors are present, you are aware of this; and when any are absent, you are aware. Moreover you are aware of how they arise.'

Maha Satipatthana Sutta 14–16

The nature of suffering

'You observe mental states in the context of the four noble truths. The first noble truth concerns suffering.

'Birth is suffering. Birth is the arising of a new form. It is the reappearance of the means of clinging to existence; and it is the re-establishing of mental activity.

'Old age is suffering. Old age is decay; it is grey hair and wrinkled skin; it is the shortening of time; it is the decline of the faculties.

'Death is suffering. Death is dropping out; it is the conclusion of a span of life; it is the dissolution of the means of clinging to existence.

'Grief is suffering. It is a state of inward sorrow and hidden misery, induced by some calamity.

'Pain is suffering. It is the consequence of bodily disease or injury; it is some form of discomfort; it is contact with that which is harmful to the body.

'Despair is suffering. It is the consequence of some misfortune; it is the result of being unable to satisfy some deep desire; it is the wish never to have been born.'

Maha Satipatthana Sutta 18

The cause of suffering

'The second noble truth concerns the cause of suffering.

'The cause of suffering is desire, which leads to rebirth. Desire is accompanied by pleasure, which is the satisfaction of desire. Desire for pleasure implies attachment to the objects of desire, and hence to life in the world, and hence to rebirth.

'Desire arises through what is pleasant to the eye, the ear, the nose, the tongue, the sense of touch, and the mind. Desire also arises through thoughts about what is pleasant to the eye, the ear, the nose, the tongue, the sense of touch, and the mind. Desire also arises through contact with what is pleasant to the eye, the ear, the nose, the tongue, the sense of touch, and the mind. Desire also arises through sensations associated with what is pleasant to the eye, the ear, the nose, the tongue, the sense of touch, and the mind.

'Desire is expressed in perceptions about what is pleasant; in intentions regarding what is pleasant; in reflections about what is pleasant, and in discussing with others what is pleasant.'

Maha Satipatthana Sutta 19

The cessation of suffering

'The third noble truth concerns the cessation of suffering.

'Suffering ceases when desire is abandoned; it ceases when the soul is free from all desire, and hence all attachment to the objects of desire.

'Desire is abandoned when you abandon what is pleasant to the eye, the ear, the nose, the tongue, the sense of touch, and the mind. Desire is also abandoned when you abandon thoughts about what is pleasant to the eye, the ear, the nose, the tongue, the sense of touch, and the mind. Desire is also abandoned when you abandon contact with what is pleasant to the eye, the ear, the nose, the tongue, the sense of touch, and the mind. Desire is also abandoned when you abandon sensations associated with what is pleasant to the eye, the ear, the nose, the tongue, the sense of touch, and the mind.

'The abandonment of desire is expressed through not perceiving what is pleasant; through having no intentions regarding what is pleasant; through not reflecting on what is pleasant; and through not discussing with others what is pleasant.'

Maha Satipatthana Sutta 20

The path leading to the cessation of suffering

'The fourth noble truth concerns the path that leads to the cessation of suffering; and this is the eightfold path of right vision, right purpose, right speech, right action, right livelihood, right effort, right awareness, and right concentration.

'Right vision consists in knowledge concerning suffering, the cause of suffering, the cessation of suffering, and the path that leads to the cessation of suffering.

'Right purpose consists in renouncing violence, and intending never to harm any living being.

'Right speech consists in refraining from speaking falsely, maliciously, harshly, and foolishly.

'Right action consists in refraining from taking life, from taking what has not been given, and from sexual immorality.

'Right livelihood consists in not profiting from deceit, fortune-telling, fraud, and exploitation.

'Right effort consists in exerting the mind so that evil and unhealthy mental states do not arise, and that good and healthy mental states do arise.

'Right awareness consists in being aware of the body, sensations, thoughts, and states of mind.'

Maha Satipatthana Sutta 21

The four stages of meditation

'Right concentration consists in entering the first stage of meditation. This requires seclusion, and brings happiness and joy. It involves thought and reflection.

'Then thought and reflection are set aside, and the second stage of meditation is entered. This leads to inner tranquillity, in which the mind is fixed on a single point. It too brings happiness and joy.

'Then happiness and joy are set aside, and the third stage of meditation is entered. This leads to total serenity, and an awareness of complete well-being.

'Then all sense of well-being and suffering is set aside, and the fourth stage of meditation is entered. This leads to utter purity of awareness.

'Those who practise the four stages of meditation for seven years, may expect two kinds of fruit. The first is perfect wisdom. The second is no further rebirth. These fruits may come after six years, five years, four, three or two years, or even one year. They may come after six months, five months, four, three or two months, or even after one month.'

Maha Satipatthana Sutta 21–22

The king's question

The Buddha was staying at Rajgir, in the mango grove belonging to the prince's tutor; with him were about twelve hundred and fifty monks. The king decided to visit the Buddha. The king bowed to the Buddha, and then sat at his side. 'I should like to put a question to you,' the king said. 'Great king,' the Buddha replied, 'you may ask whatever you wish.'

The king said: 'In my kingdom there are people engaged in all kinds of occupations, each of which requires a special skill. There are elephant drivers, horsemen, archers, cooks, barbers, bath attendants, confectioners, potters, accountants, and so on. And these people all enjoy the fruits of their labours in the form of payment. This enables them to maintain themselves and their families in comfort, and to make donations to monks and priests. Can you show what benefits are derived from the life of a monk?

'I have put this question to other spiritual leaders. One replied that there is no merit in good actions, and no loss of merit in bad actions; therefore the inaction of the monk is wiser than the action of normal people. Another replied that each soul will be reborn an allotted number of times, and that nothing can change this; and he drew the same conclusion. Another replied that at death a person is annihilated; and he drew the same conclusion. Now I put the question to you.'

Samanna-phala Sutta 1, 8, 13–15, 17–18, 20–21, 23–24, 34

From a slave to a monk

The Buddha said: 'Suppose there is a slave in your household. He rises before you do, and goes to bed after you; he is eager to do whatever you wish, and anticipates your every need. One day he reflects on the difference between your position and his; and wonders if he could earn greater merit, in order to enjoy the comforts that you do. So he escapes from your palace, shaves off his hair and beard, puts on yellow robes, and becomes a monk. He soon learns to control his actions, speech and thoughts; he is content with simple food and rough shelter; and he relishes solitude. Would you urge this man to come back to your palace as a slave?'

The king replied: 'No, I should not. On the contrary, if he came to my palace, I should greet him with reverence, standing up when he entered, and requesting him to sit down. I should offer him food, a bed, medicine, and anything else he needed, and beg him to accept. And I should give orders that he be protected.'

'Well,' the Buddha said, 'is there not some benefit in being a monk?'

The king said: 'I agree. But can you show me some other benefits from the monastic life?'

Samanna-phala Sutta 35–36

Giving up the world

The Buddha said: 'Suppose there appears in the world a teacher who is fully enlightened, whose wisdom is perfect, whose goodness is beyond measure, and who is an incomparable guide. He teaches the Way, which is beautiful at the start, beautiful throughout its progress, and beautiful at its completion. And in his teaching he shows both the spirit and the letter of truth.

'An ordinary man, living in the world, hears about this teacher, and says to himself: "Life in the world is full of anxiety and trouble, making it hard to acquire holiness. Yet the monastic life, which this teacher espouses, is free of worry, making it far easier to acquire holiness. I shall shave off my hair and beard, put on yellow robes, and become a monk." Thus he gives away his wealth, and bids farewell to his relatives.

'He is an exemplary monk. He is scrupulous in his conduct and in the food he eats; yet he is aware of the danger which lies in the avoidance of small faults. He abides by the highest principles of good action and speech; he guards the gate of his senses; he is alert and self-aware; and he is content.'

Samanna-phala Sutta 40–42

Monastic principles of action and speech

'What are these principles of good action and speech by which this monk abides?

'He avoids killing or harming any living being. He lays aside the cudgel and the sword. He never acts in a rough or uncontrolled manner. He is always merciful and compassionate.

'He never takes what has not been given; and he never grasps what is not his own. He takes only what is given, expecting that enough will be offered to meet his needs.

'He is chaste. He never has sexual intercourse.

'He never speaks a false word, and always speaks the truth; he never swerves from the truth. He is faithful and trustworthy, always keeping his promises.

'He never slanders people. What he hears from one person, he does not repeat to others; so he never stirs up quarrels. Instead he tries to bring together those who are divided, making peace wherever he can; and he chooses his words to encourage peace.

'He is never rude, avoiding harsh language. His speech is pleasant to the ear, bringing joy to the heart.

'He avoids frivolous and vain conversation. He speaks only when it is helpful; and his words are concise, conveying his meaning with clarity. Thus people remember what he has said. He finds the right illustrations to enliven his discourse.'

Samanna-phala Sutta 43–44

More monastic principles

'The monk avoids injuring plants and seeds.

'He eats only once a day. He does not eat at night, nor does he eat after midday.

'He does not go to fairs. He never watches dancers; nor does he listen to singers and musicians.

'He does not wear any kind of ornament or garland. He does not use perfumes and unguents.

'He never sleeps on a large, soft bed.

'He does not accept gifts of money. He does not accept uncooked grain or meat.

'He does not have slaves to serve him.

'He does not own sheep or goats, fowls or swine, or any kind of livestock.

'He does not ride on an elephant or a horse.

'He does not own land, whether it be fertile or waste.

'He does not act as a go-between or a messenger.

'He does not engage in buying or selling.

'A king, when he has defeated his enemies on every side, feels safe and secure. Similarly a monk, when he has learnt to live by the principles of good action and speech, feels safe and secure; he has an inner sense of comfort and ease.'

Samanna-phala Sutta 45, 63

Guarding the senses

'How does the monk guard the gate of the senses?

'When he sees an object with his eye, he does not allow himself to be overwhelmed by the beauty of its general appearance or its details. He knows that if the sense of sight is unrestrained, he will envy the owners of beautiful objects, and become dejected that he does not own them. Thus he keeps constant watch over the sense of sight.

'Similarly, when he hears a sound with his ear, or smells a fragrance with his nose, or tastes a flavour with his tongue, or feels a texture with his body, or conceives an image in his mind, he does not allow himself to be overwhelmed by the beauty of any aspect of it. He knows that if any of his senses is unrestrained, he will envy the possessors of beauty, and become dejected at his own poverty.

'As a result of watching over his senses, he experiences within himself an inner sense of comfort and ease. By guarding the gate of his senses, he knows that no evil can enter.'

Samanna-phala Sutta 64

Alertness and contentment

'How is the monk alert and self-aware?

'Whatever the monk does, he keeps in his mind's eye every aspect of his action. He considers the immediate purpose of the action. He reflects on its ethical significance. He asks whether or not it will further his ultimate spiritual aim. And he ponders the deeper nature of the action itself. He does all this when he goes out, and when he returns; when he stretches out his limbs, and when he draws them in; when he eats and drinks, masticates and swallows; when he urinates and defecates; when he stands up and sits down; when he is sleeping, and when he is walking; when he is speaking, and when he is being silent. He is constantly aware of the meaning of all he does.

'How is the monk content?

'The monk is content with sufficient robes to cover his body, and with sufficient food to keep his body alive. He is content with only those possessions that he can carry with him – just as a bird is content with its wings.'

Samanna-phala Sutta 65–66

Sitting alone

'Having learnt to live by the principles of good speech and action, having learnt to guard his senses, having become fully alert, and enjoying contentment, the monk chooses some lonely spot where he can meditate. This spot may be in a wood, at the foot of a tree; it may be a cave in a mountain; it may be on a heap of straw in a field. He returns there each morning after he has gone out begging for food. He eats the food he has been given. Then he sits cross-legged, with his body erect, and his mind concentrated.

'He sets aside all hankering for the world. He purifies himself of all desires. He suppresses any urge to injure other living beings. He frees his mind from all anger and malice. He lifts his heart and mind from torpor. He sharpens his perceptions. He banishes indolence and sloth, anxiety and worry,

irritability and vexation. He transcends confusion, perplexity and doubt.'

Samanna-phala Sutta
67–68

Images of the monk's life

'The monk is like a poor man who borrows money to start a business, which proves successful. Not only can he pay off his debt; but he also has a surplus to maintain his family in comfort. When he compares his previous situation with his present one, he is very happy.

'The monk is like a man who was suffering a painful disease, and could not digest any food, so his strength was draining away. Then he recovers from the illness, can digest food, and his strength returns. When he compares his previous situation with his present one, he is very happy.

'The monk is like a man who was held in prison, and is then set free, without even a fine. When he compares his previous situation with his present one, he is very happy.

'The monk is like a man who was a slave serving a master, unable to go where he wished. Then he is set free, becoming his own master; and he is able to go wherever he wishes. When he compares his previous situation with his present one, he is very happy.

'The monk is like a rich and prosperous man, who gets lost in the desert, with no food or water, and in great danger of attack from wild beasts. At last he reaches a village, where there is food and water, and where he is safe and secure. When he compares his previous situation with his present one, he is very happy.'

Samanna-phala Sutta 66–73

The first and second stages of meditation

'The monk now enters the first stage of meditation. In this stage of meditation his mind uses reason and logic to investigate the truth, and to detach itself from all desire. His body is drenched and permeated with the joy that comes from detachment; every part of his frame is suffused with happiness.

'Consider a skilful bath attendant. He sprinkles perfumed soap powder in a basin, and adds water drop by drop, kneading the powder into a ball of lather. The drops of water suffuse and permeate the soap. The monk is like the soap; and joy is like the water.

'This, great king, is a benefit derived from the monastic life.

'The monk now enters the second stage of meditation. All reason and logic are suppressed, and the mind concentrates on a single point. His body is drenched and permeated with the joy that comes from concentration; every part of his frame is suffused with happiness.

'Consider a deep pool, with water coming into it from a spring beneath. There is no inlet from the east or west, from the north or south; and rain never falls onto it from the sky. The cool waters from the spring suffuse and permeate the entire pool. The monk is like the pool; joy is like the spring.

'This, great king, is a benefit derived from the monastic life.'

Samanna-phala Sutta 75–78

The third and fourth stages of meditation

'The monk now enters the third stage of meditation. All joy and happiness are set aside, and the mind becomes tranquil and self-possessed; it is utterly serene. He is drenched and permeated with a sense of well-being, and suffused with serenity that transcends joy.

'Consider a lake in which there are red, white and blue lotus flowers. They do not rise above the surface of the water; and they draw nourishment from the depths of the water. The moisture suffuses and permeates the lotuses, from their tips to their roots. The monk is like a lotus; the water is like the serenity which transcends joy.

'This, great king, is a benefit derived from the monastic life.

'The monk now enters the fourth stage of meditation. All sense of well-being and suffering is set aside, and there is purity of awareness, perfect equanimity, and utter self-possession. He is drenched and permeated with equanimity, and his whole being is translucent with pure awareness.

'Consider a man wrapped from head to foot in a clean white robe. The monk is like that man; the white robe represents his purity.

'This, great king, is a benefit derived from the monastic life.'

Samanna-phala Sutta 79–82

Mental powers

'The monk now bends his mind to that wisdom that comes from truth. Through his spiritual disciplines, he understands that the body has form, that it is comprised of the four elements, that it springs from a father and a mother, that it is continually renewed by food – and that, by its very nature, it is subject to decay and disintegration. He also understands that consciousness is bound up with the body, and depends upon it.

'Think of a gem which is perfectly cut, and without flaw. It is translucent; and the eye can see within it the threads of blue or red or orange that give it colour. The monk can see his own body with the same clarity that this gem can be seen.

'Through his spiritual disciplines, the monk now possesses great mental powers. He may become many beings; and then he may become one being again. He may become invisible, and then visible again. He may walk through a wall or a mountain. He may penetrate solid ground, as if it were water; and he may walk on water, as if it were solid ground. He may cross his legs, and fly through the air like a bird; he may reach as high as the sun and the moon, touching them with his hands.

'Think of a potter, who with the power of his mind combined with the skill of his hands, can make a lump of clay into whatever shape he wants. The monk can make himself do and be whatever he wants.

'These, great king, are benefits derived from the monastic life.'

Samanna-phala Sutta 83–84, 87–88

Hearing and discernment

'Through his spiritual disciplines, the monk's hearing now surpasses normal hearing. Not only does he hear earthly sounds; he also hears celestial sounds.

'Think of a man walking along a road. He hears in the distance the sound of a drum. His hearing is so acute that he can distinguish which kind of drum is being beaten – a kettledrum, a tenor drum or a side-drum. The monk's hearing is so acute that he can hear sounds from the farthest ends of the universe, as well as the tiniest sounds from the smallest atoms on earth.

Through his spiritual disciplines, the monk can now understand the minds and moods of other living beings, including humans. He can discern the passionate mind and the calm mind; the angry mind and the peaceful mind; the dull mind and the alert mind; the attentive mind and the wandering mind; the broad mind and the narrow mind; the mean mind and the lofty mind; the steadfast mind and the wavering mind; the free mind and the enslaved mind. He recognizes each mind for what it is.

'Think of a man looking at himself in a mirror or in still water, and seeing a mole on his cheek. The monk sees the minds of others with equal clarity.

'These, great king, are benefits derived from the monastic life.'

Samanna-phala Sutta 89–92

From one existence to another

'Through his spiritual disciplines, the monk can now remember his previous existences. He recalls his last existence,
then his last but one existence, then his last but two existence, then his last but three existence, and so on, through
many aeons. As he recalls each existence, he knows his name,
his family, the type of food he ate, the pleasures he enjoyed,
the pains he suffered, and the age of his death.

'Think of a man travelling from one village to another. If
he has a good memory, he will recall his stay in each village.
He will remember the appearance of each village, to whom
he spoke there, and what was said. The monk can recall his
previous existences with equal clarity.

'Through his spiritual disciplines, the monk's vision now
surpasses normal vision. He can see beings as they pass from
one existence to another. He sees those who have acquired
merit, and so pass from a lower existence to a higher one;
and he sees those who have lost merit, and so pass from a
higher existence to a lower one.

'Think of a man standing on the roof of a tall house in
the middle of a town. With keen eyesight he can see people
leaving one house, and going into another. The monk can
see people passing from one existence to another with equal
clarity.

'These, great king, are benefits derived from the monastic
life.'

Samanna-phala Sutta 93–96

Perfect knowledge

'Through his spiritual disciplines, the monk now knows the four noble truths for himself. He knows suffering, as it really is. He knows the cause of suffering, as it really is. He knows the cessation of suffering, as it really is. And he knows the path that leads to the cessation of suffering, as it really is. Through this knowledge the soul is set free from sensuality and from ignorance; and the soul knows its salvation. The soul knows that rebirth has been destroyed, the spiritual life has been fulfilled, and the purpose of all existence has been accomplished.

'Think of a high mountain, at the top of which is a pool of water. The water is perfectly clear and perfectly still. A man standing on the bank looks into the water. With his keen eyesight he sees oysters, pebbles, and shoals of fish; he sees everything in the pool. The monk knows truth as clearly as that man knows the content of the pool.

'This, great king, is the supreme benefit derived from the monastic life.'

Samanna-phala Sutta 97–98

The king's confession

When the king had heard the Buddha's discourse, he exclaimed: 'Spiritual master, that is excellent. It is as if someone has restored a building which lay in ruins. It is as if someone had found a precious gem which had been hidden. It is as if someone had shown the right road to a traveller who was lost. It is as if someone had brought a bright lamp into a dark room. Your simple images and metaphors have enabled me to see the truth. I beg you to be my teacher, accepting me as your disciple. Today I submit myself to your guidance; and I shall obey you until the day I die. But first I must confess my great sin. I have been weak, foolish and wrong. My father was a good man and a just ruler; but for the sake of acquiring his power, I murdered him. Do not turn me away; help me to control myself in the future.'

The Buddha replied: 'You have indeed committed a great sin. But in confessing it you have acted righteously. I accept your confession. Those who look upon their faults, and know them to be faults, are able to control themselves in the future.'

The king rose, bowed to the Buddha, and went back to his palace. When the king had gone, the Buddha turned to his monks, and said: 'If the king had not murdered his father, then this very day, as he sat here with me, he would have attained enlightenment.'

Samanna-phala Sutta 99–102

Evil conduct and its motives

The Buddha was staying near Rajagaha in the bamboo garden.
Early one morning a young man from Rajagaha, called Sigala,
came out from the city to the bamboo garden. He bathed in
a pool, wetting his hair and his garments. Then he rose out
of the pool, lifted his arms above his head, and clasped his
hands together. He bowed to the east, to the south, to the
west, and to the north.

   The Buddha saw the young man, and asked him what he
was doing. Sigala replied: 'When my father was dying, he
commanded me each morning to worship the four quarters
of the earth. So I am honouring my father's word.' The
Buddha said: 'You should not worship the four corners of the
earth in this manner.' 'How should I worship them?' Sigala
asked. 'Young man,' the Buddha said, 'pay attention, and I
shall tell you.'

   The Buddha and the young man sat down side by side,
and the Buddha spoke: 'To worship the four quarters of the
earth, you must first put aside the four kinds of evil conduct.
These are destruction of life, taking what is not given, sexual
misconduct, and telling lies. To do this you must suppress the
four motives which lead to evil conduct. These are partiality,
hatred, stupidity and fear. If you succeed in suppressing these
motives, you will not engage in evil conduct.'

Sigalavada Sutta 1–5

Dangers of the world

The Buddha continued: 'There are six ways of dissipating wealth; and, if you wish to worship the four quarters of the earth, they must be avoided. They are being addicted to intoxicating liquors; going out late at night; visiting fairs; gambling; having dissolute friends; and being habitually idle.

'There are six dangers associated with being addicted to intoxicating liquors. These are loss of wealth; quarrelling; susceptibility to disease; loss of reputation; indecent exposure; and impaired intelligence.

'There are six dangers from going out late at night. These are being attacked by robbers; your wife at home being attacked by robbers; your children at home being attacked by robbers; your property being taken by robbers; being suspected of crime; and being the subject of false rumours.

'There are six dangers from visiting fairs. These are obsession with the sight of dancing; obsession with the sound of singing; obsession with the sound of music; obsession with the amusement of dramas; obsession with the clash of cymbals; and obsession with the beat of drums.'

Sigalavada Sutta 7–10

More dangers of the world

'There are six dangers from gambling. These are winning, and thereby inducing hatred in those who lose; losing, and thereby mourning the loss of wealth; becoming poor and destitute through continuously losing; being regarded as untrustworthy; being despised by both friends and officials; and being regarded as unsuitable for marriage.

'There are six dangers from having dissolute companions. These are being drawn into gambling; being drawn into sexual misconduct; being drawn into drinking intoxicating liquors; being drawn into cheating; being drawn into crime; and being drawn into brawls and other violent activities.

'There are six dangers from being habitually idle. These are feeling the heat, in order to claim excessive heat as an excuse for not working; feeling the cold, in order to claim excessive cold as an excuse for not working; feeling the hour is too early, in order to claim the earliness of the hour as an excuse for not working; feeling the hour is too late, in order to claim the lateness of the hour as an excuse for not working; feeling hungry, in order to claim hunger as an excuse for not working; and becoming poor and destitute, through failing to earn anything.'

Sigalavada Sutta 11–13

Unsuitable friends

'There are four kinds of people who should be regarded as unsuitable friends: those who are rapacious; those who prefer words to deeds; those who flatter; and those who are self-indulgent.

'There are four reasons for shunning rapacious people: they take much; they give little; they act not out of duty, but out of fear; and they pursue only their own interests.

'There are four reasons for shunning those who prefer words to deeds: they exaggerate their past good deeds; they over-estimate their future good deeds; they try to gain favour with empty promises; and when you need help, they will find excuses for not giving it.

'There are four reasons for shunning flatterers: they agree with you, even when you are wrong; you cannot tell when they think you are right; they praise you to your face; and they speak ill of you behind your back.

'There are four reasons for shunning those who are self-indulgent: they encourage you to drink intoxicating liquors with them; they encourage you to go out at night with them; they encourage you to visit fairs with them; and they encourage you to gamble with them.'

Sigalavada Sutta 15–19

Suitable friends

'There are four kinds of people who should be regarded as suitable friends: those who are helpful; those who are the same in happiness and adversity; those who offer wise advice; and those who are sympathetic.

'There are four reasons for cherishing helpful people: they guard you when you are off guard; they guard your property when you are off guard; they protect you when you are frightened; and they support you when you are in need.

'There are four reasons for cherishing those who are the same in happiness and adversity: they tell you their secrets; they keep your secrets; in times of trouble they do not abandon you; they are willing to risk life and limb for your sake.

'There are four reasons for cherishing those who offer wise advice: they restrain you from doing wrong; they encourage you to do what is right; they share their insights with you; and they point you towards enlightenment.

'There are four reasons for cherishing those who are sympathetic: they do not rejoice over your bad fortune; they rejoice over your good fortune; they restrain others from speaking ill of you; and they encourage others to speak well of you.'

Sigalavada Sutta 21–25

Parents, teachers, spouse and friends

'Each of the four quarters of the earth should be regarded as a symbol: the east symbolizes parents; the south symbolizes teachers; the west symbolizes one's spouse; and the north symbolizes friends and companions.

'There are four ways in which you should treat your parents: you should show gratitude for their work in raising you; you should care for them in their old age; you should strive to continue the family line; and you should strive to make yourself worthy of your heritage.

'There are four ways in which you should treat your own children: you should love them; you should seek to restrain them from vice; you should encourage them towards virtue; and you should train them for a profession.

'There are four ways in which you should treat your teachers: you should rise to greet them; you should serve them; you should be eager to learn; and you should be attentive when they teach.

'There are four ways in which you should treat your spouse: with love; with courtesy; with fidelity; and with respect for her wisdom.

'There are four ways in which you should treat your friends and companions: with generosity; with compassion; with consideration; and with loyalty.'

Sigalavada Sutta 27–31

Roaring like lions

The Buddha was staying at Savatthi. He summoned his monks, and addressed them: 'When you speak to monks belonging to other communities, roar like lions. When they ask you why you are roaring like lions, give them four reasons. The first is that you have confidence in your teacher. The second is that you have confidence in his teaching. The third is that he has given moral precepts covering all situations. The fourth is that he regards all people, monks and lay people alike, with compassion.

'The monks from other orders may say that they too have confidence in their teacher and his teachings; that he has given moral precepts covering all situations; and that he regards all people with compassion.

'Then ask them whether there is one final goal, or are there many final goals. If they answer correctly, they will say there is one final goal.

'Then ask them whether a person attaining the final goal has attachment, or does not have attachment. If they answer correctly, they will say the person does not have attachment.'

Culasihanada Sutta: Majjhima Nikaya 1.64–65

The correct answers

'Then ask the monks from other orders whether a person attaining the final goal has ill will, or does not have ill will. If they answer correctly, they will say the person does not have ill will.

'Then ask them whether a person attaining the final goal has delusive ignorance, or does not have delusive ignorance. If they answer correctly, they will say the person does not have delusive ignorance.

'Then ask them whether a person attaining the final goal has desire, or does not have desire. If they answer correctly, they will say the person does not have desire.

'Then ask them whether a person attaining the final goal is intelligent, or is not intelligent. If they answer correctly, they will say the person is intelligent.

'Then ask them whether a person attaining the final goal is strong-willed, or is weak-willed. If they answer correctly, they will say the person is strong-willed.

'Then ask them whether a person attaining the final goal is indolent and distracted, or is diligent and concentrated. If they answer correctly, they will say the person is diligent and concentrated.'

Culasihanada Sutta: Majjhima Nikaya 1.65

Eternal life and annihilation

'In some communities the monks are taught to believe in eternal life after death; in some they are taught to believe in annihilation.

'Those who believe in eternal life, cannot understand the notion of annihilation. Those who believe in annihilation, cannot understand the notion of eternal life.

'Yet both these beliefs are spiritually dangerous. Those who believe in eternal life, become attached to this notion; they desire eternal life; and they hate the notion of annihilation. Thus by believing in the notion of eternal life, they remain bound to the wheel of birth, death, and rebirth. Equally those who believe in annihilation, become attached to this notion; they desire annihilation, and they hate the notion of eternal life. Thus by believing in the notion of annihilation, they remain bound to the wheel of birth, death, and rebirth.

'You must thus be free from attachment either to the notion of eternal life, or to the notion of annihilation. You should desire neither eternal life nor annihilation. Thus you will break free from the wheel of birth, death, and rebirth.'

Culasihanada Sutta: Majjhima Nikaya 1.66

Four forms of grasping

'There are four forms of grasping: the grasping of pleasure;
the grasping of beliefs; the grasping of religious rituals; and
the grasping of the notion of self.

'The monks of most communities, although they pretend
to understand all the four forms of grasping, in fact only understand one. In some communities the monks only understand the grasping of pleasure; in some the monks only
understand the grasping of beliefs; in some they only understand the grasping of rites and rituals; and in some they only
understand the grasping of the notion of self. In all these
communities the teacher and his teachings are shown not to
be perfect; the teacher is manifestly not enlightened, and so
his teachings are flawed.

'What is the cause of these graspings? Desire is the cause.
What is the cause of desire? Sensual feeling is the cause of
desire. What is the cause of sensual feeling? Contact with
external objects is the cause of sensual feeling. What is the
cause of contact with external objects? Each of the senses is
the cause of contact with external objects. What is the cause
of each of the senses? Consciousness is the cause of each of
the senses. What is the cause of consciousness? Delusive
ignorance is the cause of consciousness.

'When the monk has shattered delusive ignorance, he no
longer grasps pleasure, beliefs, religious rituals, and the notion of self. And thereby he attains nirvana.'

Culasihanada Sutta: Majjhima Nikaya 1.67

Expelling evil thoughts

The Buddha was staying at Savatthi. He summoned his monks, and addressed them: 'From time to time an image or thought enters your mind which is evil. It is associated with desire, or with hatred, or with illusion, or with ignorance. Then you must generate in your mind an image which is good. This good image will drive away the evil image; so the mind becomes calm, compassionate, aware, and concentrated.

'A builder uses a slender peg to knock out and remove a thicker one. In the same way, you should use a good mental image to knock out and remove a bad one.

'But if an evil image or thought continues to disturb your mind, you must generate in your mind deep loathing for this image; and you must reprimand yourself for having it. You should come to regard the evil image with utter horror.

'A young man or woman might feel pleasure in wearing some beautiful ornament round the neck. But if that ornament were replaced with a lump of rotting meat, the young man or woman would react with disgust, and tear it off. Although an evil image may seem beautiful, you should regard it as a lump of rotting flesh.'

Vitakkasanthana Sutta: Majjhima Nikaya 1.118–120

Destroying evil thoughts

'If an evil image or thought continues to disturb your mind, you should resist that thought with constant determination, slowing eroding it.

'A man running swiftly may ask himself why he is hurrying; and if he can think of no good reason, he may decide to walk slowly. Later he may ask himself why he is walking; and if he can think of no good reason, he may decide to stand still. Later he may ask himself why he is standing; and if he can think of no good reason, he may decide to sit down. Later he may ask himself why he is sitting; and if he can think of no good reason, he may decide to lie down. Thus he gradually discards more vigorous postures, and adopts gentler ones. In the same way you can gradually destroy an evil image, and adopt a good one.

'If an evil image persists in disturbing your mind, you should fight it with clenched teeth and with your tongue pressed against the palate. By this means you will finally destroy it; and your mind will become calm, compassionate, aware, and concentrated.

'By these means you may become master of your own thoughts. Whatever thoughts you wish to think, you will think; and whatever thoughts you do not wish to think, you will not think.'

Vitakkasanthana Sutta: Majjhima Nikaya 1.120–121

Learning forbearance

The Buddha was staying at Savatthi, with his monks and nuns. A young monk, called Phagguna, used to stay in the company of the nuns beyond the proper time. And whenever any other monk spoke critically of the nuns, Phagguna exploded with rage, defending the nuns with great passion. One of the monks reported Phagguna's behaviour to the Buddha; and the Buddha summoned Phagguna.

The Buddha asked Phagguna if the report were true; and Phagguna confessed that it was. Then the Buddha said: 'Phagguna, you came from a noble family, and you joined this community out of faith. Therefore it is quite improper for you to mix with the nuns beyond the proper time. And when someone speaks critically of the nuns, you should suppress all passionate emotions, as these belong to the life of the world. If passionate emotions begin to rise; you should say to yourself: "My mind will not be perverted, and I shall not utter angry, hateful words. I shall hold only good thoughts in my mind, and look upon everyone with love and good will." Even if someone threatened to hit the nuns with a stick, you should still say these words to yourself. Moreover, if someone speaks critically of you, then you should also say these words to yourself. And if one person threatens to hit another person with a stick, you should say these words. In this way you will learn the virtue of forbearance.'

Kakacupama Sutta: Majjhima Nikaya 1.122–123

One meal a day

The Buddha then turned to his monks, and addressed them:
'As I have said to you before, you should take only one meal
a day. As a result of taking one meal a day, I am free from
disease, and free from any chronic ailment; I am active, and
I have great strength. If you restrict yourselves to one meal a
day, you too will be free from diseases and ailments, and you
will remain active and strong. But I have no need to say this;
you know it already, and abide by it.

'Consider a chariot yoked with pedigree horses. A chariot-
eer could steer the chariot wherever he wanted, without
using the whip. In the same way, if you cultivate good habits,
you will have complete control over the body.

'Consider a forest of sal trees, which is undergrown with
castor-oil plants. A man takes over the management of the
forest. He cuts down the saplings which are twisted and de-
formed, leaving only those which are healthy. And on the
trees he cuts off the branches that are crooked and misshapen.
In this way the forest becomes healthy and luxuriant. In the
same way, cut out what is bad in your lives, and devote yourselves to developing what is good.'

Kakacupama Sutta: Majjhima Nikaya 1.124

A ruined reputation

The Buddha told a story: 'In this town of Savatthi there was a housewife, called Videhika. She was reputed to be gentle, humble and calm. She had a servant, called Kali, who was industrious and efficient. One day Kali thought: "Although my mistress is reputed to be gentle, humble and calm, she surely has a temper. She does not show it because I do my work so well. What if I were to test my mistress?"

'The next morning Kali rose late from bed. Videhika asked her the reason for her lateness. "No reason in particular," Kali replied. Videhika frowned. The following morning Kali rose even later from bed. Vedehika asked her the reason. "No reason in particular," Kali replied. Videhika scowled. The following morning Kali rose later still from bed. Vedehika asked her the reason. "No reason in particular," Kali replied. Videhika flew into a rage, and shouted at Kali. Then she pulled the bolt from a door, and hit Kali with it. Kali ran from the house, with blood trickling down her face, and told neighbours what Videhika had done. As a result Videhika's reputation was ruined.

'Like Videhika, you are all reputed to be gentle, humble and calm. But how would you react if you were tested? Suppose that you did not get the food, the clothes and the medicines you need. Would you still be gentle, humble and calm? The only means of remaining gentle, humble and calm at all times is to follow the Way.'

Kakacupama Sutta: Majjhima Nikaya 1.125–126

Five aspects of speech

'Speech has five aspects. It may be timely or untimely. It may be truthful or untruthful. It may be gentle or harsh. It may be reasonable or unreasonable. It may convey good will or ill will. Suppose someone speaks to you in an untimely manner; or they are untruthful; or they are harsh; or they are unreasonable, or they convey ill will. Then you should say to yourself: "My mind will not be perverted, and I shall not utter angry, hateful words. I shall hold only good thoughts in my mind, and look upon everyone with love and good will."

'Suppose a man tried to dig up the earth with a spade. Would he succeed in destroying the earth? No, because the earth is too deep; he would merely make himself tired and weary. In the same way, do not let those who attack you with words, succeed in destroying you.

'Suppose a man tried to paint the sky. Would he succeed in changing the colour of the sky? No, because the sky is too wide; he would merely make himself tired and weary. In the same way, do not let those who attack you with words, succeed in destroying you.

'Suppose a man tried to evaporate the river Ganges with a torch. Would he succeed in making the river dry? No, because the river is too great; he would merely make himself tired and weary. In the same way, do not let those who attack you with words, succeed in destroying you.'

Kakacupama Sutta: Majjhima Nikaya 1.126–127

The Buddha's decision to become a monk

The Buddha was staying in Savatthi. One day some of his monks went to visit a priest called Rammaka. The priest invited them into his house, where they talked for many hours. Eventually the Buddha himself went to Rammaka's house. He waited outside until there was a lull in the conversation; then he knocked on the door. The monks opened the door, and he entered.

'What was the subject of your talk?' the Buddha asked. 'We were talking about you,' the monks replied. So the Buddha began speaking about himself: 'When I was young, I understood that I was a slave to suffering. I realized that I was subject to old age, illness, death, grief and corruption. And I wondered if it were possible to break free from suffering – to break free from the cycle of birth, death and rebirth.

'At that time I was extremely handsome, with jet black hair. I shaved off my hair, and put on the yellow robes of a monk. My parents were very upset, and wept profusely. But despite their tears I left my home, and began to wander from place to place. I was searching for the state of spiritual peace which is beyond understanding – the state of nirvana.'

Ariyapariyesana Sutta: Majjhima Nikaya 1.160–161, 163

Two spiritual teachers

'I went to the spiritual teacher Alara Kalama, and asked for
his guidance. He began to guide me, and I soon understood
his teaching. The purpose of his teaching was to guide souls
to the sphere of nothingness. I myself entered this sphere. I
then asked him if he had anything more to teach. He replied
that he had not; and he invited me to share with him the
leadership of his community. I felt honoured by this invitation. But it occurred to me that entering the sphere of nothingness does not lead to detachment, cessation of suffering,
serenity, truth, enlightenment and nirvana. Thus I left Alara
Kalama.

'Then I went to Uddaka Ramaputta, and asked for his
guidance. He began to guide me, and I soon understood his
teaching. The purpose of his teaching was to guide souls
to the sphere where there is neither perception nor non-
perception. I myself entered this sphere. I then asked him if
he had anything more to teach. He replied that he had not;
and he invited me to share with him the leadership of his
community. I felt honoured by this invitation. But it occurred
to me that entering the sphere where there is neither perception nor non-perception, does not lead to detachment, cessation of suffering, serenity, truth, enlightenment and nirvana.
Thus I left Uddaka Ramaputta.'

Ariyapariyesana Sutta: Majjhima Nikaya 1.163–166

Cessation of perception

'Thus I continued to search for the state of spiritual peace which is beyond understanding – the state of nirvana. Eventually I came to the village of Senani at Uruvela. There I found a delightful forest, with a river of clear water flowing through it. There was a ford across the river. So I decided to sit in seclusion on the far side of the river; and come back to the village each day for food.

'While I was there, I attained enlightenment; and I knew that at the end of this life I shall enter nirvana. Thus I broke free from all suffering – from old age, illness, death, grief and corruption. I broke free from the cycle of birth, death and re-birth. I realized that my final birth had already occurred, and that I had no future bodily life to endure.

'By my own spiritual exertions I learnt that enlightenment is beyond the sphere of nothingness; and it is beyond the sphere where there is neither perception nor non-perception. It is the sphere where there is cessation of perception, and hence cessation of all attachment.'

Ariyapariyesana Sutta: Majjhima Nikaya 1.166–167, 175

Attitudes to food

While the Buddha was staying in Rajagaha, a physician called
Jivaka came to him, and said: 'I have heard that animals are
deliberately killed to provide meat for you. Is this true or
false? And what are your views on the eating of meat?'

The Buddha replied: 'Those who say that animals are
killed to provide meat for me, are speaking falsely. A monk
should never eat meat from animals which have been killed
for him. Even if the monk only suspects this, and does not
have certain knowledge, he should reject the meat.

'When a monk is invited by a layman for a meal, the
monk gives no thought to the quality of the food he will eat.
He has no desire for food; he does not brood over it; he is
not in any way attached to it. On the contrary, he is aware
of all the suffering and misery associated with food. It is in
this frame of mind that he eats the meal offered to him.'

Jivaka Sutta: Majjhima Nikaya
1.368–369

A double-edged question

The local ruler, called Abhaya, went to Nataputta, a monk who belonged to a community hostile to the Buddha. Nataputta said to Abhaya: 'If you were to defeat Gautama, whom they call the Buddha, in public debate, your reputation would be hugely enhanced.' Abhaya said: 'How can I defeat Gautama in debate? His power is too great, and his ability is too vast.'

Nataputta said: 'Go to Gautama, and ask him this question: "Would an enlightened person ever utter words which were disagreeable and unpleasant to others?" If he replies that an enlightened person would speak in such a way, say to him: "Then there is no difference between an enlightened person and an ordinary person; ordinary people frequently utter words which are disagreeable and unpleasant to others." But if he replies that an enlightened person would never speak in such a way, say to him: "Then you cannot be enlightened; you said that your cousin and enemy Devadutta will suffer for an aeon, and your words made him angry."'

Nataputta continued: 'Thus, when you ask this double-edged question, Gautama will be unable either to spew it out or to swallow it. It will be as if a piece of barbed iron were stuck in his throat.'

Abhaya agreed to this plan; and he immediately went to the Buddha. He invited him for a meal the following day, with the intention of asking the question afterwards.

Abhayarajakumara Sutta: Majjhima Nikaya 1.392–393

The Buddha's principles for speech

The Buddha came to Abhaya's palace the following day; and
the prince served the Buddha himself, giving him the finest
food. Then after the meal Abhaya asked the Buddha: 'Would
an enlightened person ever utter words which were disagreeable and unpleasant to others?' The Buddha said, 'Is not this
question double-edged?' Abhaya exclaimed: 'Nataputta and
his community are already defeated.' The Buddha asked:
'Why do you say that?' Abhaya told the Buddha that Nataputta had urged him to ask that question, in order to defeat
him in debate.

A little boy was lying beside Abhaya, with his head on the
ruler's knee. The Buddha said: 'If that little boy had a stone
stuck in his throat, what would you do?' Abhaya replied: 'Out
of compassion for the boy, I should put my finger down his
throat and pull the stone out – even if I drew blood.'

The Buddha said: 'I never utter falsehood. If I know something to be true, but nobody would benefit from hearing it,
and some would be hurt, I do not utter it. If I know something to be true, and some would benefit from hearing it, and
others would be hurt, I wait for the right time to utter it. If
I know something to be true, but nobody would benefit from
hearing it, though some would find it pleasant, I do not utter
it. If I know something to be true, and some would benefit
from hearing it, and some would find it pleasant, I utter it.'

Abhayarajakumara Sutta: Majjhima Nikaya 1.393–395

Answering questions

Abhaya asked the Buddha: 'When people come to you with a spiritual question, do you pause for reflection, only answering the question when you have had ample time to consider it? Or do you answer the question at once?'

The Buddha said: 'Let me answer your question by questioning you. Are you an expert in the construction of chariots?' Abhaya replied that he was. The Buddha continued: 'When people come to you with a question about chariots, do you pause for reflection, only answering the question when you have had ample time to consider it? Or do you answer the question at once?' Abhaya replied: 'Since I know everything about chariots, I am able to answer at once.' The Buddha said: 'And since I know the ultimate truth, I am able to answer spiritual questions at once.'

On hearing this reply, Abhaya begged the Buddha to accept him as a disciple.

Abhayarajakumara Sutta: Majjhima Nikaya 1.395–396

The danger of waves

The Buddha and his monks were staying near Catuma. He summoned his monks, and addressed them: 'When people wade or swim in a large river, there are four dangers: the danger of waves; the danger of crocodiles; the danger of whirlpools; and the danger of big fish. Similarly those who leave home and abandon their possessions, and embrace the monastic life, face four dangers – which are symbolized by the four dangers of going into a river.

'What does the danger from waves symbolize? Imagine a man from a wealthy, noble family deciding to become a monk. The reason for his decision is to put an end to suffering. He joins a community, and the other monks are constantly instructing him on his conduct. They tell him when he should go out, and when he should return; they tell him in which directions he should look; they tell him when to draw in his legs, and when to stretch them out; they tell him how he should tie his robes; they tell him how he should hold his bowl – and so on. The man says to himself: "When I was at home, I used to give instructions to others. Now in this community I receive instructions from people whose families are much inferior to my own." So he gives up being a monk, and returns to his former life.

'This man may be said to have been overwhelmed by waves – which symbolize despair originating in anger.'

Catuma Sutta: Majjhima Nikaya 1.456, 459–460

The danger of crocodiles

'What does the danger of crocodiles symbolize? Again, imagine a man from a wealthy, noble family deciding to become a monk. The reason for his decision is to put an end to suffering. He joins a community, and the other monks are constantly instructing him on his diet. They tell him what he may eat, and what he may not eat; how much of each food he may eat, and how much is regarded as excessive; what he may drink, and what he may not drink; when he may eat and drink, and when he may not eat and drink – and so on. The man says to himself: "When I was at home, I could eat whatever I wanted, in whatever quantities I wanted; I could drink whatever I wanted, in whatever quantities I wanted; and I could eat and drink whenever I wanted. Now in this community a check is put on everything that goes into my mouth." So he gives up being a monk, and returns to his former life.

'This man may be said to have been overcome by crocodiles – which symbolize gluttony.'

Catuma Sutta: Majjhima Nikaya 1.460–461

The danger of whirlpools

'What does the danger of whirlpools symbolize? Again, imagine a man from a wealthy, noble family deciding to become a monk. The reason for his decision is to put an end to suffering. He joins a community, and has to rise early in the morning; he has to take his bowl, and go into a nearby village or town, begging for food; he has to watch over all that he does and says; and he has to restrain his senses. In every village and town he sees young men enjoying themselves; far from restraining their senses, they are indulging their senses to the full. The man says to himself: "When I was at home, I too used to indulge my senses to the full. My family possesses great wealth. So it was possible for me both to enjoy the wealth, and to perform many acts of charity, thereby gaining great merit." So he gives up being a monk, and returns to his former life.

'This man may be said to have been overcome by whirlpools – which symbolize indulgence of the senses.'

Catuma Sutta: Majjhima Nikaya 1.461

The danger of big fish

'What does the danger of big fish symbolize? Again, imagine a man from a wealthy, noble family deciding to become a monk. The reason for his decision is to put an end to suffering. He joins a community, and each day goes into a nearby town or village, begging for food. He frequently sees both young women and older women. Some are completely covered by their robes, while others are dressed quite scantily. Sexual passion rises up into his mind, and fills it. He says to himself: "If I abandoned the monastic life, I could satisfy my sexual desires. I could engage in whatever sexual activity I wished." So he gives up being a monk, and returns to his former life.

'This man may be said to have been overcome by big fish – which symbolize the objects of sexual desires.

'Thus there are four dangers which are constantly faced by those who leave home, and abandon their possessions. So be constantly vigilant.'

Catuma Sutta: Majjhima Nikaya 1.462

Breathing and the body

The Buddha was staying in Savatthi. One evening, when the moon was full, at the end of the four months in which the white water lily blossoms, he addressed his monks in the open air: 'You should develop awareness of your breathing, both your inhaling and your exhaling. Awareness of inhaling and exhaling is vital in learning the four forms of contemplation, and in making the seven links of enlightenment. So how is it developed?

'You should find a secluded place, perhaps in a forest at the foot of a tree, where you can be sure of not being disturbed.

'When you are breathing in a long breath, you should think: "I am breathing in a long breath." When you are breathing out a long breath, you should think: "I am breathing out a long breath." When you are breathing in a short breath, you should think: "I am breathing in a short breath." When you are breathing out a short breath, you should think: "I am breathing out a short breath."

'Next, as you breathe in, you should think: "As I breathe in, I am aware of my whole body." And as you breathe out, you should think: "As I breathe out, I am aware of my whole body."

'Next, as you breathe in, you should think: "As I breathe in, I calm the activities of the body." And as you breathe out, you should think: "As I breathe out, I calm the activities of the body."'

Anapanassati Sutta: Majjhima Nikaya 3.78–79, 82

Breathing and the mind

'Next, as you breathe in, you should think: "As I breathe in, I am aware of joy." And as you breathe out, you should think: "As I breathe out, I am aware of joy."

'Next, as you breathe in, you should think: "As I breathe in, I am aware of my mind." And as you breathe out, you should think: "As I breathe out, I am aware of my mind."

'Next, as you breathe in, you should think: "As I breathe in, I calm the activities of my mind." And as you breathe out, you should think: "As I breathe out, I calm the activities of my mind."

'Next, as you breathe in, you should think: "As I breathe in, I compose my mind." And as you breathe out, you should think: "As I breathe out, I compose my mind."

'Next, as you breathe in, you should think: "As I breathe in, I concentrate my mind." And as you breathe out, you should think: "As I breathe out, I concentrate my mind."

'Next, as you breathe in, you should think: "As I breathe in, I free my mind." And as you breathe out, you should think: "As I breathe out, I free my mind."'

Anapanassati Sutta: Majjhima Nikaya 3.82–83

Breathing and reflection

'Next, as you breathe in, you should think: "As I breathe in, I reflect on the impermanence of all things." And as you breathe out, you should think: "As I breathe out, I reflect on the impermanence of all things."

'Next, as you breathe in, you should think: "As I breathe in, I reflect on detachment from all things." And as you breathe out, you should think: "As I breathe out, I reflect on detachment from all things."

'Next, as you breathe in, you should think: "As I breathe in, I reflect on the extinction of sensuality." And as you breathe out, you should think: "As I breathe out, I reflect on the extinction of sensuality."

'Next, as you breathe in, you should think: "As I breathe in, I reflect on the extinction of desire." And as you breathe out, you should think: "As I breathe out, I reflect on the extinction of desire."

'Next, as you breathe in, you should think: "As I breathe in, I reflect on the extinction of illusion." And as you breathe out, you should think: "As I breathe out, I reflect on the extinction of illusion."

'Next, as you breathe in, you should think: "As I breathe in, I reflect on the extinction of ignorance." And as you breathe out, you should think: "As I breathe out, I reflect on the extinction of ignorance."'

Anapanassati Sutta: Majjhima Nikaya 3.83

The four aspects of contemplation

'Now you are ready to engage in the four aspects of contemplation.

'The first is contemplation of body. You are full of energy; your consciousness is clear; your mind is alert; you have overcome all misery. You contemplate breathing as a phenomenon of body.

'The second is contemplation of sensation. You are full of energy; your consciousness is clear and alert; you have overcome all misery. You contemplate breathing as a phenomenon of sensation.

'The third is contemplation of mind. You are full of energy; your consciousness is clear and alert; you have overcome all misery. You contemplate breathing as a phenomenon of mind.

'The fourth is contemplation of mental objects. You are full of energy; your consciousness is clear and alert; you have overcome all misery. You contemplate breathing as a phenomenon of mental objects.'

Anapanassati Sutta: Majjhima Nikaya 3.84

The seven links of enlightenment

'Now you are ready to make the seven links of enlightenment.

'When you are deep in contemplation of body, sensation, mind, and mental objects, you may make the link of self-awareness.

'When you are deep in contemplation of body, sensation, mind, and mental objects, you may make the link of searching for truth.

'When you are deep in contemplation of body, sensation, mind, and mental objects, you may make the link of energy.

'When you are deep in contemplation of body, sensation, mind, and mental objects, you may make the link of joy.

'When you are deep in contemplation of body, sensation, mind, and mental objects, you may make the link of serenity.

'When you are deep in contemplation of body, sensation, mind, and mental objects, you may make the link of concentration.

'When you are deep in contemplation of body, sensation, mind, and mental objects, you may make the link of equanimity.'

Anapanassati Sutta: Majjhima Nikaya 3.85–86

Differences at birth

The Buddha and his monks were staying near Savatthi. A young man, called Subha, came to the Buddha, and asked: 'Why are some people born with many blessings, and some born with few blessings? Why do some people suffer frequent illness, while others are free from sickness? Why are some people ugly, and others beautiful? Why are some people poor, and others rich? Why are some born into families of low social standing, and others into families of high social standing? Why are some people lacking in intelligence, while others possess great intelligence?'

The Buddha replied: 'People inherit what they are from the past. Their past deeds are really their ancestors. Their past deeds determine their present condition.' Subha said: 'I cannot understand what you are saying. I beg you to explain the Way in words which I can understand.'

The Buddha said: 'Listen carefully to what I say. Consider a woman or a man who kills and injures other living beings without restraint. That person's present life may be short; and after death that person will be reborn in a body which will suffer frequent injury.

'Consider a woman or a man who refrains from killing or injuring any other living being. That person's present life may be long; and after death that person will be reborn in a body which will never be injured.'

Culakammavibhanga Sutta: Majjhima Nikaya 3.202–203

The consequences of cruelty and anger

'Consider a woman or man who takes pleasure in cruelty
to other living beings, tormenting them in body and mind.
That person's present life may be short; and after death that
person will be reborn in a body which will be subject to
much sickness.

'Consider a woman or a man who refrains from cruelty to
other living beings. That person's present life may be long;
and after death that person will be reborn in a body which is
free from sickness.

'Consider a woman or a man who is angry and irritable;
when that person is blamed or criticized, even mildly, the reaction is an explosion of rage. That person's present life may
be short; and after death that person will be reborn in a body
which is ugly.

'Consider a woman or a man who is never angry or irritable; when that person is blamed or criticized, the reaction
is to listen calmly to what is said. That person's present life
may be long; and after death that person will be reborn in a
body which is beautiful.

Culakammavibhanga Sutta: Majjhima Nikaya 3.204

The consequences of envy and meanness

'Consider a woman or a man who is envious of the wealth, honour and respect that others enjoy. That person's present life may be short; and after death that person will be reborn with no power.

'Consider a woman or a man who is never envious of the wealth, honour and respect that others enjoy. That person's present life may be long; and after death that person will be reborn with great power.

'Consider a woman or a man who is mean and stingy, never giving food to the hungry, drink to the thirsty, or support to monks and priests. That person's present life may be short; and after death that person will be reborn into poverty.

'Consider a woman or a man who is kind and generous, freely giving food to the hungry, drink to the thirsty, and support to monks and priests. That person's present life may be long; and after death that person will be reborn into wealth.

Culakammavibhanga Sutta: Majjhima Nikaya 3.204–205

The consequences of pride and stubbornness

'Consider a woman or a man who is proud and conceited, never rising to greet people, never honouring those who deserve honour, and treating common people with contempt. That person's present life may be short; and after death that person will be reborn into a family of low social standing.

'Consider a woman or a man who is humble and modest, always rising to greet people, honouring those who deserve honour, and treating all people with courtesy. That person's present life may be long; and after death that person will be reborn into a family of high social standing.

'Consider a woman or a man who is stubborn and close-minded, and refuses to ask for advice and guidance from people of wisdom. That person's present life may be short; and after death that person will be reborn with little wisdom.

'Consider a woman or a man who is open-minded, and eagerly asks for advice and guidance from people of wisdom. That person's present life may be long; and after death that person will be reborn with great wisdom.'

The Buddha concluded: 'This explains why some people are born with many blessings, and some people are born with few. That is why I say that people inherit what they are from the past. Their past deeds are really their ancestors. Their past deeds determine their present condition.'

Culakammavibhanga Sutta: Majjhima Nikaya 1.205–206

Monks in cold water

The Buddha and his monks were staying near Gaya. Staying nearby were monks from a sect which practised the most extreme austerities. It was winter, and snow was falling. At dawn each morning monks from this austere sect plunged in and out of the river, and splashed each other. They believed that in doing this they attained spiritual purity.

One morning the Buddha led his own monks to the bank of the river to observe this activity. Then he turned to his monks, and said: 'It is not by pure water that the soul is made pure; the soul is purified by truth. It is not by austerities that a person becomes holy; it is by following the Way.'

Udana 1.9

Hitting a snake

The Buddha was staying near Savatthi. One morning, as he
was walking into the city to beg for food, he observed a
group of boys hitting a snake with a stick.

When he returned, he summoned his monks, and told
them about the incident. Then he said: 'The snake wants happiness, as much as any man or woman does. The snake wants
to be saved from suffering, as much as any man or woman
does. Those who themselves want happiness, and yet cause
suffering to other living beings, will not themselves find happiness. Those who themselves want happiness, and cause no
suffering to other living beings, will indeed find happiness for
themselves.

Udana 2.3

Taking oil

Living in the city was a lazy, dishonest priest, whose wife was pregnant. His wife said to him one morning: 'Go and fetch some oil, which I shall use at my delivery.' The priest did nothing. The next morning she repeated her request. So the priest went to the king's storehouse, and took some oil. But on his way home he drank the oil himself. Soon afterwards he was seized by a terrible pain in his belly, and writhed on the ground in agony.

As the Buddha was walking to the city to beg for food, he saw the man writhing on the ground. Later he summoned his monks, and related the incident. Then he concluded: 'Those who own nothing themselves, are truly happy. Those with the highest knowledge, own nothing. Those who take what they want, are truly miserable. Those with the deepest ignorance, take much.'

Udana 2.6

Five hundred beautiful women

Ananda, the Buddha's cousin and closest disciple, said to a group of his fellow monks: 'I am unhappy. I cannot continue with the monastic life. I shall give up this spiritual training, and return home.'

One of those who heard these words, reported them to the Buddha. So the Buddha summoned Ananda, and asked him why he was unhappy. Ananda replied: 'Whenever I go into the city to beg for food, I see a beautiful young woman. She is the most beautiful woman in the land. As I pass, she looks up, and says: "May you return soon." I cannot continue to lead the monastic life, when my mind is filled with her image.'

The Buddha took Ananda by the arm, and told him to close his eyes. 'What do you see?' the Buddha asked. 'I see five hundred beautiful young women,' Ananda replied. The Buddha asked: 'How do they compare with the young woman you see on your way to the city?' 'They are even more beautiful than she is,' Ananda replied. The Buddha said: 'If you remain a monk, all those women will be yours.'

Ananda decided to remain a monk. When he told the other monks of his vision of five hundred women, and the Buddha's promise that they would be his, they mocked him. Their mocking humiliated him; and in his humiliation, he saw his folly. That evening he went to the Buddha, and said: 'Today you promised me five hundred beautiful women. I hereby release you from that promise.'

Udana 3.2

Loving yourself

One evening the king and queen were sitting on the roof of their palace. The king asked his queen: 'Is there anyone dearer to you than you yourself?' The queen replied: 'In all truth there is no one dearer to me than myself. Is there anyone dearer to you than you yourself?' The king replied: 'In all truth there is no one dearer to me than myself.'

The king decided to go to the Buddha at once, and relate to him this conversation, asking for his comment. The Buddha said: 'If you investigate all external objects, you will find than none is dearer to you than you yourself. If you investigate all other living beings, you will find than no one is dearer to you than you yourself. When you understand this, you truly love yourself. And those who truly love themselves, never deliberately cause injury to others.'

Udana 5. 1

A flame at night

One dark night the Buddha was sitting with his monks in the open air, with an oil lamp burning beside him. He observed the lamp as insects flew into its flame, and destroyed themselves.

The Buddha then said: 'Those insects see the flame, and misunderstand it. They imagine that it offers them life and happiness; but in truth it means misery and death. In the same way human beings see bright flames: the bright flame of wealth; the bright flame of power; the bright flame of honour and fame. They rush towards those flames, thinking that they offer life and happiness – only to find that they bring misery and death. So turn away from what you see and hear outside yourselves; and turn inwards to your own mind and soul.'

Udana 6.9

The condition of nirvana

While he was staying near Savatthi, the Buddha summoned his monks, and spoke to them about nirvana: 'There is that condition where there is no earth, no water, no fire and no air. This condition is not the sphere of the infinity of space; it is not the sphere of the infinity of consciousness; it is not the sphere of nothingness; it is not the sphere in which there is neither perception nor non-perception; it is not in this world, nor in another world, nor in the sun, nor in the moon. In this condition there is neither coming nor going; there is neither staying nor leaving; there is neither being born nor dying. In this condition there is neither stillness nor movement. In this condition there is the cessation of all suffering.

'In this condition there is no self; and that which is without self, is hard to understand. In this condition there is no falsehood; and where there is no falsehood, the truth is hard to see. Only those who have extinguished all desire, can understand lack of self; only those who have extinguished all attachment, can see truth.

'In this condition there is no instability, and yet there is no support for what is unstable. In this condition there is serenity; and where there is serenity, there is no coming and going; and where there is no coming and going, there is no being born and dying; and where there is no being born and dying, it is neither here nor elsewhere. In this condition there is the cessation of all suffering.'

Udana 8.1, 2, 4

A people's strength

The Buddha was staying in Rajgir. At that time the King of
Magadha had made up his mind to attack the Vajjian people,
in order to uproot and destroy them. He called his chief
minister Vassakara, and said to him: 'Go to the Buddha, bow
down at his feet, and ask after his health. Then tell him that
I, the King of Magadha, am eager to attack the Vajjians. Listen
to the Buddha's response. Whatever the Buddha predicts will
be fulfilled, because the Buddha can speak nothing untrue.'

So Vassakara went to the Buddha, and told him of the
King's desire to attack the Vajjians. The Buddha replied:
'There are various reasons why we may expect the Vajjians to
prosper, and not decline. They assemble frequently to discuss
matters of common concern. They argue vigorously, without
becoming hostile to one another. They are open to reason, so
their arguments always reach a decision on which everyone
can agree. They implement their decisions with great determination. They treat their elderly members with respect,
seeking their advice. They have many shrines in their land, at
which they perform with great diligence the ancient rituals.
They honour men and women who have devoted their lives
to the acquisition of wisdom. For all these reasons we may
expect the Vajjians not to decline, but to prosper.'

Vassakara said: 'I take this to mean the King should not
attack them.' 'As you say,' the Buddha said. Vassakara rose
and left.

Maha Parinibbana Sutta 1.1–5

Conditions for the Community to prosper

The Buddha summoned his monks, and addressed them: 'There are seven conditions which must be fulfilled, if the Community is to flourish. The monks should frequently gather together. They should meet in a spirit of unity. They should decide nothing contrary to that which has already been established. They should honour the senior members of the Community, listening carefully to their advice. They should not allow desire to influence their discussions. They should each take delight in solitude. And each should exercise unceasing control over his mind. If these conditions are fulfilled, you may expect the Community not to decline, but to prosper.

'There are seven further conditions which must be fulfilled, if the Community is to flourish. The monks should not be connected with any form of commerce. They should not engage in any kind of idle talk. They should never be indolent. They should never attend social gatherings. They should not allow themselves to be motivated by malice. They should not make friends with those who habitually do evil. They should keep their attention firmly fixed on their ultimate goal. If these conditions are fulfilled, you may expect the Community not to decline, but to prosper.'

Maha Parinibbana Sutta 1.6–7

Further conditions for the Community

'There are seven further conditions which must be fulfilled, if the Community is to flourish. Monks should be faithful, modest, conscientious, studious, diligent and vigilant; and, above all, they should strive for wisdom. If these conditions are fulfilled, you may expect the Community not to decline, but to prosper.

'There are seven further conditions which must be fulfilled, if the Community is to flourish. In particular, monks should make the seven links of enlightenment. They should be self-aware; they should search for the truth; they should be energetic; they should be joyful; they should be serene; their minds should be concentrated; and they should have equanimity. If these conditions are fulfilled, you may expect the Community not to decline, but to prosper.

'There are seven further conditions which must be fulfilled, if the Community is to flourish. Monks should engender within themselves the perception of: the impermanence of things; the non-existence of the ego; the ugliness of the world; suffering in the world; the value of detachment; the value of renouncing passion; the cessation of suffering. If these conditions are fulfilled, you may expect the Community not to decline, but to prosper.'

Maha Parinibbana Sutta 1.7–10

Conditions for the harmony of the Community

'There are six conditions that must be fulfilled, if the monks are to live in harmony. The monks should be kind to one another in action, speech and thought, both in public and in private. They should share all things, even including the food they receive in their begging bowls. They should practise all virtues, since every virtue contributes to the salvation of the soul; it is for this reason that virtues are praised by the wise.

'The monks should do nothing that, if it were known, would tarnish the public reputation of the Community. They should value one another's spiritual insights, since every insight may contribute to the salvation of the soul. And they should strive for the cessation of suffering, in themselves and in others. If these conditions are fulfilled, you may expect the Community not to decline, but to prosper.'

Maha Parinibbana Sutta 1.11

Morality, meditation and wisdom

Some time later the Buddha summoned his monks and nuns again, and spoke to them about morality, meditation and wisdom. He said: 'It is useless for you to meditate, if you lead an immoral life; meditation without morality brings no spiritual fruit. But if the context of your meditation is a moral life, then you will enjoy great spiritual fruit.

'It is useless to acquire spiritual wisdom, if you lead an immoral life; knowledge without morality does not bring wisdom. But if the context of your acquisition of knowledge is a moral life, then you will become truly wise.

'A mind that is wise can never be intoxicated by sensual desires; it can never be intoxicated by the beauties and pleasures of the world; it can never be intoxicated by personal opinions and by intellectual debate; and it can never be intoxicated by ignorance.'

When the Buddha had finished speaking, he announced that he and his monks and nuns should leave Rajgir, and go to Ambalatthika.

Maha Parinibbana Sutta 1.12–13

The Buddha's greatness

The Buddha stayed at Ambalatthika with his Community for a short time, and then they moved to Nalanda, where they stayed in a mango grove. One evening Sariputta came to see the Buddha, and declared: 'I believe there never has been, and never will be, a man who is greater and wiser than you!'

The Buddha said: 'You speak grandly and boldly, Sariputta. Have you known many other spiritual masters? Have you questioned them deeply, and observed them closely?' 'No,' replied Sariputta. The Buddha asked: 'Do you know the full extent of my wisdom?' 'No,' replied Sariputta. The Buddha asked: 'Can you see into the past with such clarity, that you know a person of greater spiritual stature has never existed; and can you see into the future with such clarity, that you know a person of greater spiritual stature never will exist?' 'No,' replied Sariputta.

The Buddha asked: 'So why do you speak so grandly and so boldly?' Sariputta replied: 'Because you have taught me the Way that leads to nirvana.'

Sariputta continued: 'A king builds a city on the border of his kingdom. It has high, thick walls, with watchtowers at each corner, and only one gate. At the gate is a watchman who can distinguish those who are loyal to the king, from those who are not; and he only allows the king's loyal subjects to enter. Each evening he walks around the walls. He sees many crevices, and observes even the tiny animals that go in and out. Through you I have become like that watchman.'

Maha Parinibbana Sutta 1.16–17

The consequences of immorality

When the Buddha had stayed at Nalanda for a short time, he
led his monks and nuns to Pataligama. A number of men and
women at Pataligama, who were lay disciples of the Buddha,
invited him to stay in the village guest house. When he accepted their invitation, they spread fresh sand on the floor of
the guest house, and put a water-pot and an oil-lamp there.

That evening the people of Pataligama assembled outside
the guest house, and the Buddha addressed them: 'Householders, breaking the moral law brings five kinds of suffering.
In the first place, immoral people lose all sense of purpose,
and become listless and lethargic; this leads to indolence,
which in turn causes poverty. Secondly, immoral people are
unpopular amongst their neighbours. Thirdly, immoral people, when they find themselves in the company of good and
honest people, feel ashamed and confused. Fourthly, immoral
people are frightened of death. Fifthly, immoral people know
that after death they will suffer the full consequences of their
evil behaviour.'

Maha Parinibbana Sutta 1.19–21, 23

The consequences of morality

The Buddha continued: 'Just as breaking the moral law brings
five kinds of suffering, so obeying the moral law brings five
kinds of benefits. In the first place, moral people have a
strong sense of purpose, which endows them with great energy; thus they work hard, and earn a good living. Secondly,
moral people are popular amongst their neighbours. Thirdly,
moral people are confident of themselves in any company,
knowing that they deserve the respect of all. Fourthly, moral
people have no fear of death. Fifthly, moral people look forward to dying, knowing that after death they will enjoy the
full consequences of their good behaviour.'

When he had finished speaking about morality, the
Buddha said: 'It is now late, and you must go home.' He
went back into the guest house, and began to meditate.

Maha Parinibbana Sutta

1.24–25

Spiritual forces

The King of Magadha had sent two ministers to Pataligama,
to organize the building of a fortress against the Vajjian people. With his clear and supernatural vision the Buddha could
see many spiritual forces haunting the site of the fort. He said
to Ananda, his cousin and closest disciple: 'Pataligama will
become a great city, where merchants will conduct every kind
of trade. But three dangers will hang over it: that of fire; that
of water; and that of dissension among friends.'

The king's ministers came to visit the Buddha, and invited
him and his monks to eat with them. The Buddha accepted
their invitation; and with their own hands they served the
Buddha with boiled rice and sweet cakes.

After the meal the Buddha spoke to the two ministers
about the fort they were building. He informed them that
they had chosen the particular site because strong spiritual
forces drew them there. And he warned them to treat those
spiritual forces with respect: 'If you revere them, they will revere you. If you honour them, they will honour you. If you
are gracious to them, they will treat you as a mother treats
her only son. By this means you will enjoy good fortune.'

The Buddha rose from his seat, and walked down to the
river Ganges, which was so full it was almost bursting its
banks. He watched people rowing across the river in boats
and rafts, and said: 'If they knew the Way, they would not
need earthly vessels.'

Maha Parinibbana Sutta 1.26—34

Destiny after death

The Buddha led his monks to Kotigama. There he gave an address about the four noble truths, and concluded: 'If you do not truly understand these truths, you have a long journey to make, going from one birth to the next, with much suffering. But once you understand them, the journey is over, and all suffering ceases.'

The Buddha then led his Community to Nadika. There was a plague raging there, and a large number of the monks and nuns died. Ananda came to the Buddha, and asked what was the destiny of their dead companions. The Buddha replied: 'The brother Salha destroyed all the intoxicants which affect the soul – sensual desire, material pleasure, personal opinion, and ignorance – and so attained nirvana. The sister Nanda broke all the fetters which bind the soul to this world, and so attained nirvana. Sugata broke many of those fetters – in particular, greed, hate and delusion – but not all; and so must return for one more birth before attaining nirvana.' The Buddha also mentioned the others who had died, saying that some had already attained nirvana, while some would return to earthly life once more.

The Buddha concluded: 'There is nothing strange in death; human beings are dying at every moment. I could tell you the destiny of each one; but this would be very dull and wearisome for me.'

Maha Parinibbana Sutta 2. 1–3, 5–8

A mirror of truth

A short time later the Buddha again spoke to Ananda: 'Lay disciples of the Buddha may have complete confidence in their teacher. They may be certain that he is fully enlightened, that his wisdom is perfect, that his joy is complete, that he understands the mysteries of the universe, and that he is a master of the soul. In the Buddha they possess a mirror of the truth.

'Lay disciples of the Buddha may have complete confidence in the Community of monks and nuns which he founded. They may know that those who follow the Buddha's teachings, are walking on the right path. Thus they may know that the Community is worthy of food and shelter, and worthy of respect. And they may know that by supporting the Community, they acquire merit. In the Community they possess a mirror of the truth.'

Soon afterwards the Buddha left Nadika, and led his Community to Vesali. They stayed in the mango grove belonging to a courtesan called Ambapali, and they ate at her house. When the wealthy people of Vesali learnt where the Buddha was staying and eating, they were extremely angry, believing that they should have had the honour of entertaining him.

Maha Parinibbana Sutta 2.9, 11, 14–16

The first illness

The rainy season was now about to begin. The Buddha told his monks and nuns to spend the season in and around Vesali, seeking accommodation with relatives and friends. The Buddha himself went to the nearby village of Beluva, accompanied by some of the senior monks, including his closest companion Ananda. He stayed at the house of a wealthy disciple.

As the rains began, the Buddha became very ill, with sharp pains running through his body, as though he were about to die. He bore the pains without complaint. The thought occurred to him: 'It would be wrong to die without addressing my disciples, and taking leave of my Community. I must make a great effort to overcome this illness, and remain alive until the appropriate time has come.' So he exerted his will over his body, and the illness subsided.

When he felt sufficiently strong, the Buddha came out of the house, and sat under a tree. Ananda came and sat beside him. 'Dear lord,' Ananda said, 'when I observed you falling ill, I too felt ill. My body weakened, my vision became blurred, and my mind fell into confusion. But I took comfort in the thought that you would not die until you had left instructions concerning the Community.'

Maha Parinibbana Sutta 2.22−24

The pains of old age

The Buddha said to Ananda: 'As I approach death, I wonder what the Community expects of me. I have taught the Way. Some teachers pretend that certain aspects of spiritual knowledge are esoteric, and can only be imparted to particular privileged people; but I have made every aspect of spiritual knowledge plain, and hence available to everyone. Other teachers have closed fists, whereas my fists are open.

'Perhaps there are certain monks who secretly want to lead the Community – who want the Community to become dependent on them. Let them declare openly their ambitions and plans. I myself have taken no pleasure in exercising leadership, and I have no wish for the Community to be dependent on me. So why should I leave instructions for the future?

'Ananda, I am old and full of years, and my earthly journey is drawing to a close. I have reached the sum of my days; I have turned eighty years of age. Like a worn-out carriage that can only be kept together with bits of rope, by body is kept together with bandages. I am only comfortable when my soul is so deep in meditation that I cannot feel any bodily sensations.'

                                    Maha Parinibbana Sutta 2.25

A lamp and a refuge

'You are to be lamps for yourselves. You are to be a refuge for yourselves. Do not seek any external refuge. Hold firmly to the Way as your lamp. Hold firmly to the Way as your refuge. Do not look to anyone besides yourselves as a refuge.

'A monk is a lamp for himself. A monk is a refuge for himself. He does not need an external refuge. Let him hold firmly to the Way as his lamp. Let him hold firmly to the Way as his refuge. He should not look to anyone besides himself as a refuge.

'Be vigilant and energetic. Be self-aware and reflective. Suppress both desire and despair. Watch over your sensations, thoughts and states of mind.

'Both now and after I am dead, let the Community be a lamp for itself. Let the Community be a refuge for itself. It should not seek any external refuge. May it hold firmly to the Way as its lamp. May it hold firmly to the Way as its refuge. It should not look to anyone outside itself as a refuge.

'Those who understand these words, will transcend darkness – but they must remain eager to learn.'

Maha Parinibbana Sutta 2.26

Spiritual abilities

One morning the Buddha went with Ananda to a shrine near Vesali. The priest of the shrine put out a mat for them, and they sat down.

The Buddha said: 'In the course of my life I have acquired many spiritual powers. I can discern future events. I know what people are thinking and feeling, regardless of whether they express their thoughts and feelings in words. I can recall my own past lives, and also the past lives of others. I became aware of these abilities after I attained enlightenment; and since that time I have learnt how to exercise them to perfection. I could use these abilities to remain alive on earth for many years and aeons.'

At that moment Ananda should have begged the Buddha to remain on earth, for the spiritual welfare and happiness of all people. But Ananda did not understand what the Buddha was saying, and so he said nothing. The Buddha repeated his words a second and a third time; and Ananda still did not understand. So the Buddha said to Ananda: 'Leave me for a while, and do whatever you want.' 'As you say, lord,' Ananda replied, and went to sit under a tree a short distance away.

Maha Parinibbana Sutta 3. 1–6

The decision to die

Soon after Ananda had left, the Devil came to the Buddha and stood beside him. The Devil said: 'It is time for you to die; you should die now. Your purpose has been fulfilled. Your monks and your nuns, and also your lay disciples, both male and female, have heard your teachings and learnt them by heart. They follow the precepts which you have laid down; and they convey to others your message. Every word you have spoken has been remembered, and is discussed in great depth. So your work is complete. There is no purpose in your staying alive any longer. So die at once.'

The Buddha said to the Devil: 'You can relax! I shall die soon. Within three months I shall be dead.' With these words the Buddha deliberately rejected the remaining years of his natural life; and his body and mind filled with joy. At that moment the earth began to tremble, and the sky rumbled with thunder.

Maha Parinibbana Sutta 3.7–10

Possible causes of the earthquake

Ananda ran over to the Buddha, to ask why the earth was trembling and the sky rumbling. The Buddha replied: 'There are eight possible causes. The earth rests on water, the water rests on wind, and the wind rests on space. When the mighty winds blow, they shake the waters, which in turn shake the earth. This is the first possible cause.

'An enlightened man or woman of great spiritual power, who has all passions and desires under total control, may meditate on the tiniest portion of earth and the widest expanse of water, and thereby understand the comparative value of things. Such meditation may make the waters shake and the earth move. This is the second possible cause.

'A soul which has attained nirvana, may decide to return to earth by entering the womb of a woman; and the earth may shake at the magnitude of this event. This is the third possible cause.

'A soul which has attained nirvana, having entered a woman's womb, may decide to depart; and the earth may shake violently at the magnitude of this event. This is the fourth possible cause.'

Maha Parinibbana Sutta 3.12–16

Further possible causes of the earthquake

'An individual, after following the eightfold path, may come to understand the four noble truths, and thereby attain perfect enlightenment; and the earth may shake violently at the magnitude of this event. This is the fifth possible cause.

'An individual, after following the eightfold path, may come to understand the four noble truths, and then found a community of righteousness; and the earth may shake violently at the magnitude of this event. This is the fifth possible cause.

'An individual who has attained enlightenment, may decide to reject the remainder of the natural span of life, and die at once; and the earth may shake violently at the magnitude of this event. This is the seventh possible cause.

'An individual who has attained enlightenment actually dies, and is not reborn, thereby breaking free from the cycle of death and rebirth; and the earth may shake violently at the magnitude of this event. This is the eighth possible cause.'

Maha Parinibbana Sutta 3.17–20

Reflections on preaching

'I have attended many kinds of gathering, of many different
kinds of people: of kings and noblemen, of priests and
monks, and of ordinary householders. In each case I have
adopted their style of speech, and I have even changed the
colour of my skin. Then I have been able to preach to them
in a manner which they can understand. By this means I have
guided and encouraged them, filling them with gladness.

'After I had finished, they often asked: "What kind of
being can inspire in such a way? Is he human or divine?"
Then I have vanished from their sight, leaving them to ask:

"What kind of being
can vanish from sight
in this way? Is he
human or divine?"'

Maha Parinibbana Sutta
3.21–22

Overcoming the delusion of permanence

'Ananda,' the Buddha continued, 'most people are deluded by the apparent permanence of external objects. There are eight stages of overcoming this delusion.

'The first stage is to become aware that the mind perceives external forms.

'The second stage is to become aware that the mind perceives the body as a form external to itself.

'The third stage is to recognize that all forms are figments of the mind.

'The fourth stage is to pass beyond the concept of finite forms, to the concept of infinite space.

'The fifth stage is to pass beyond the concept of infinite space, to the concept of infinite mind.

'The sixth stage is to pass beyond the concept of infinite mind, to the concept of nothingness.

'The seventh stage is to pass beyond the concept of nothingness, to the concept that concepts are nothing.

'The eighth stage is to pass beyond the concept that concepts are nothing, to the cessation of all concepts.'

Maha Parinibbana Sutta 3.24, 33

Ananda's pleading

The Buddha continued: 'Soon after I attained enlightenment, the Devil came to see me, and said: "It is time for you to die; you should die now." But I resisted the Devil. I told him that I should remain in this body for many years, teaching people the truth, and giving people precepts by which they may lead good lives. And I committed myself to remain alive until enough people understood the truth, that every false teacher could be refuted.

'The Devil came to me again a short time ago, and again urged me to die. On this occasion I told him to relax, assuring him that I should be dead within three months.'

Ananda said: 'Dear lord, I beg you to remain alive on earth for many years and aeons, for the spiritual welfare and happiness of all people. Stay on earth out of compassion for the world!' The Buddha replied: 'The time for entreaties is past.' Ananda begged a second time, and again the Buddha rebuffed him. Ananda pleaded with the Buddha a third time, and the Buddha said: 'It seems that you have no faith in my wisdom.' 'Of course I have faith in your wisdom.' Ananda replied. 'Then why do you trouble me three times?' the Buddha said.

Maha Parinibbana Sutta 3.34–39

The separation of death

Ananda persisted: 'Lord, I have heard you speak about the spiritual abilities that a person acquires on attaining enlightenment. And you have said that an enlightened person can use these abilities to remain on earth for many years and aeons. You have learnt how to exercise these abilities to perfection. Therefore you could choose to stay on earth.'

The Buddha said: 'You are repeating what I said to you a short while ago; but you did not then understand my meaning. If at that time you had pleaded with me to remain on earth, I should have rejected your plea initially. If you had repeated your plea, I should still have rejected it. But if you had repeated it again, I should have granted it. In failing to do this, you did wrong.'

The Buddha continued: 'As I have said many times to you, we are all destined to be separated from those whom we love; all friendships must end. That which is born and comes into existence, will inevitably dissolve and die at some time.'

The Buddha then ordered Ananda to summon the monks. When they had assembled, he said: 'My body is now ripe, and my life draws to a close. I leave you the refuge which I have made. Be earnest; be vigilant; keep yourselves pure; be determined; watch over your minds; hold firmly to all I have taught you. Then you will never again be reborn; your suffering will end.'

Maha Parinibbana Sutta 3.40, 48–49, 51

The four principles

The following morning the Buddha went with Ananda from
Beluva, the village where they were staying, into Vesali to beg
for food. His neck and back were now stiff, so he turned as
an elephant does, swivelling his whole body at once. After
they had eaten, the Buddha said to Ananda: 'This is the last
time I shall see Vesali.'

The Buddha then summoned his Community, and he led
them to the village of Bhandagama. That evening he addressed the monks and nuns: 'Each of us has wandered wear-
ily from one life to another for many thousands of years,
being born and dying and then being reborn. We have been
forced to make this long journey because we have failed to
understand and grasp the four principles. What are these four
principles?

'The first is noble morality; the second is noble meditation; the third is noble wisdom; and the fourth is noble salvation. When these four principles are realized and known,
then all that leads to future existence, is rooted out, and there
is no further birth. When these four principles are realized
and known, then suffering comes to an end.'

Maha Parinibbana Sutta 4. 1—2

The test of truth

After a few days at Bhandagama, the Buddha led his monks
and nuns to Bhoganagara. There he again addressed them: 'A
monk may at any time quote words which he has heard from
my mouth. My words should not be received with praise, nor
should they be treated with scorn. Those who recall them and
hear them, should simply try to understand them. If, however, a monk claims that I have uttered certain words, but
these words do not accord with the basic tenets of my teaching, you should conclude that his claim is false.

'A monk may at any time quote words which he has heard
from the mouths of senior members of the Community.
These words should not be received with praise, nor should
they be treated with scorn. Those who recall them and hear
them, should simply try to understand them. If, however, a
monk claims that senior members have uttered certain words,
but these words do not accord with the basic tenets of my
teaching, you should conclude that his claim is false.'

Maha Parinibbana Sutta 4.8–9

Unclean meat

The Buddha led his Community to Pava, where they stayed
in a mango grove belonging to a blacksmith called Chunda.
When Chunda heard that that Buddha had arrived, he invited
the Buddha and his monks to eat at his house. He prepared a
large quantity of rice, cakes and tender pork.

When the Buddha and his Community arrived, the Buddha
asked for the pork to be served to him, and for the rice and
cakes to be served to the monks. When he had eaten a small
portion of the pork, the Buddha said to Chunda: 'Please take
away the rest of this pork, and bury it in a hole. Such meat
is so unclean that it would kill any normal person who ate
it.' 'As you say, lord,' Chunda replied; he took the pork outside, and buried it immediately.

That evening the Buddha fell ill with acute dysentery, suffering sharp pains in his abdomen which he endured without complaint. The next morning the Buddha announced that
he and the Community should move on to Kusinara.

Maha Parinibbana Sutta 4.13–15, 17–20

Making muddy water clean

On the journey to Kusinara the Buddha left the road, and leaned against a tree. He said to Ananda: 'Spread out your robe for me. I am very weary, and must rest for a while.' Ananda folded his robe in four, and spread it on the ground. The Buddha sat down on it.

Then the Buddha, pointing to a nearby stream, said: 'I am thirsty. Fetch me some water.' Ananda replied: 'Just now several carts have crossed the stream, stirring up the bed. So the water is very muddy. Let me carry you to another river, where the water is clear and pure. There you can quench your thirst, and also cool your limbs.' But the Buddha again said: 'I am thirsty. Fetch me some water.'

Ananda protested a second time, but the Buddha was insistent. So Ananda went to the nearby river, carrying the Buddha's bowl. To his astonishment the water was clear and pure. He cried out: 'How great is my master's power! He can make muddy water clean.' He filled the Buddha's bowl with water, and took it back to him. The Buddha drank his fill, and then rose up to continue the journey.

Maha Parinibbana Sutta 4.21–25

Inhaling faith

Later in the afternoon a young man, called Pukkusa, was walking along the road in the opposite direction. Pukkusa was a disciple of Alara Kalama, a spiritual teacher whom the Buddha had rejected in his search for enlightenment. Seeing the Buddha, Pukkusa bowed, and said: 'My master was once seated under a tree by a road, when five hundred carts came by. His head and body were covered with the dust which they threw up. Yet he was meditating so deeply that he was utterly unaware of them: he neither saw nor heard them. That demonstrates that he attained a wonderful state of inner calm.'

The Buddha said: 'Which do you think is more difficult: remaining undisturbed by the sound of five hundred carts passing by; or remaining undisturbed by the sound of a violent thunderstorm?' The Buddha then explained how his teaching gave people such inner calm, that nothing could disturb them. At the end Pukkusa said: 'This very moment I blow away my faith in Alara Kalama, and inhale a new faith – in Gautama Buddha.'

Pukkusa was extremely wealthy, and wished to show his new allegiance to the Buddha with a precious gift. So he went into a nearby town, and purchased two robes made from gold thread. He then presented them to the Buddha, saying: 'I beg you to do me the honour of accepting these.' The Buddha replied: 'Put one of the robes on me, and the other on Ananda.' Pukkusa did as the Buddha ordered.

Maha Parinibbana Sutta 4.26–28, 33–35

Anticipating nirvana

When Pukkusa had left, Ananda took off the robe which he had received, and put it on the Buddha, so the Buddha was now wearing both robes. Ananda stood back to look at the Buddha, and said: 'It is strange that when these robes are put on you, they seem to lose their splendour. The clarity and brightness of your complexion makes them seem dull by comparison.'

The Buddha replied: 'There are two occasions when the complexion of a holy man or woman is especially clear and bright. The first occasion is on the night when enlightenment is attained. The second occasion is when the enlightened person is about to pass into complete nirvana.'

The Buddha led his monks and nuns down to the river Kakuttha. He waded into the water, and bathed his entire body. Then he climbed onto the bank, and lay down on his right side, with one foot resting on the other.

After meditating for a short time, he said to Ananda: 'I am concerned that, when I die, Chunda the blacksmith will be overwhelmed by remorse. He will know that the last food I ate was his pork, and that this made me ill; so he will blame himself for my death. So after I have died I want you to go to Chunda, and say: "It is to your credit that you gave the Buddha his last meal, and he himself asked me to express his gratitude to you. The meal he ate at your house hastened his passage to nirvana."'

Maha Parinibbana Sutta 4.37–38, 42

Places of pilgrimage

The Buddha led his Community to Kusinara, on the far side
of the river Hiranyavati; and they stayed in a grove of sal
trees. The Buddha said to Ananda: 'I beg you to make a couch
for me between two sal trees, with its head to the north. I
am very weary, and wish to lie down.' Ananda did as the
Buddha asked; and the Buddha lay down. At that time the
sal trees were covered with blossom, and petals fell on the
Buddha.

Ananda said to the Buddha: 'During your lifetime the
members of your Community and your many lay disciples
have frequently come to visit you, wherever you happen to
have been. When you have died, where can members of your
Community and your lay disciples visit you?'

The Buddha replied: 'There are four places which people
should visit with feelings of reverence. The first is the place
where I was born. The second is the place where I attained
enlightenment. The third is the place where I first taught the
Way. And the fourth is this place, where I shall die and enter
nirvana. Those who visit these places with feelings of reverence will earn great merit, and will be reborn to a higher
state.'

Maha Parinibbana Sutta 5. 1–2, 7–8

Plans for the Buddha's remains

Ananda asked the Buddha: 'What are we to do with your bodily remains?' The Buddha replied: 'Do not hinder your spiritual progress with such a concern. Devote yourself to your own good. There are many wealthy lay disciples – noblemen, merchants and priests – who will want to honour my remains. Let them do so.'

But Ananda persisted: 'We need your instructions about what should happen to your bodily remains.' The Buddha replied: 'My remains should be treated in the same way as people treat the remains of a universal monarch.' 'How, lord, do they treat the remains of a universal monarch?' Ananda asked. The Buddha replied: 'They wrap the body of a universal monarch in a new cloth. They put cotton wool round it, and wrap it again in a new cloth. They continue doing this until there are five hundred layers of cloth and cotton wool. They lift the body into an iron vessel filled with oil; and they lift that vessel into another iron vessel filled with oil. They place it on a funeral pyre which has been sprinkled with every kind of perfume, and set it alight. Earth is heaped over the ashes to make a burial mound, which is cased in brick. This is how the body of a universal monarch is treated. My body should be treated in the same fashion.'

Maha Parinibbana Sutta 5.10–11

Visiting the burial mound

The Buddha continued: 'Ananda, there are four types of people who are worthy of having a burial mound built over their ashes. The first is an enlightened person who teaches others. The second is an enlightened person who remains silent. The third is a true disciple of an enlightened person. The fourth is a universal monarch. When people visit the burial mounds of such people, their hearts are made calm and happy.'

As Ananda listened to the Buddha, he began to weep, saying to himself: 'I am only a learner, who is still very far from attaining enlightenment. Who will care for me when my teacher dies and enters nirvana?'

'Ananda,' the Buddha said, 'do not grieve in this fashion. As I have said many times to you, we are all destined to be separated from those whom we love; all friendships must end. That which is born and comes into existence, will inevitably dissolve and die at some time. For many years, Ananda, you have served me with devotion, and your mind has been filled with love for me. Your service has been constant, and your love has been beyond measure. Continue to strive for salvation with all your strength – and soon you will attain it.'

Maha Parinibbana Sutta 5.12–14

Ananda's qualities

The Buddha now addressed the whole Community: 'All the Buddhas of past ages had companions who served them with unstinting devotion – just as Ananda has served me. Ananda is a man of great wisdom. He has controlled the flow of people coming to visit me. He has known the right time for each monk and nun to seek my advice. He has welcomed kings and noblemen, as well as ordinary householders; and he has made them wait until I was ready to receive them, and they were ready to hear my words. Ananda is also a great teacher. When people come to visit him, his appearance fills them with joy. When he speaks about the Way, his discourse fills them with joy. And when he is silent, people feel ill at ease.'

Ananda said to the Buddha: 'You should not die in this small town built of wattle and daub – in this insignificant place in the middle of the jungle. In your lifetime you have stayed in many great cities, such as Rajgir, Savatthi, Kosambi and Isipatana. And in all those places you have numerous disciples, including many wealthy noblemen and priests, who would treat your bodily remains with great honour.' 'Ananda,' the Buddha replied: 'Do not speak of Kusinara in such a foolish manner.'

Maha Parinibbana Sutta 5.15–17

The leaders of Kusinara

'Now, Ananda,' the Buddha said, 'go into the town, and tell the leaders that I shall die in the last hour of the night. I do not want them to reproach themselves afterwards, saying: "The Buddha died near our town, and we did not go and see him in his last hours."'

Ananda went into Kusinara, and delivered the Buddha's message to the leaders, begging them to take notice of it. The leaders were distressed to hear of the Buddha's imminent death, as were their wives and children. Many of them wept and dishevelled their hair. Some fell prostrate on the ground, and rolled to and fro in the dust, crying out in anguish: 'It's too soon for the Buddha to die! It's too soon for the eye of the world to vanish from us!' Then they all set out for the sal grove where the Buddha and his Community were staying.

As they walked, Ananda said to himself: 'If I allow each of the leaders one by one to pay their respects to the Buddha, it will be dawn before they have finished.' So when they arrived at the sal grove, he ordered them to form themselves into groups, and he presented them to the Buddha group by group.

Maha Parinibbana Sutta 5.19–23

Testing spiritual teachers

At that time a monk called Subhadda was living in Kusinara. In the course of his life he had listened to many spiritual teachers; but he had not put his faith in any of them, because he doubted their wisdom. When he heard that the Buddha was nearby, he decided to go and visit him, in the hope that he would find in him true wisdom.

When Subhadda reached the sal grove, he begged Ananda to allow him to see the Buddha. But Ananda replied: 'The Buddha is weary, and on the point of death. You cannot trouble him now.' The Buddha overheard this exchange, and called out to Ananda: 'Do not stop Subhadda. He comes from a genuine desire for knowledge, so he will not annoy me. And whatever I say to him, he will quickly understand.' So Ananda allowed Subhadda to approach the Buddha, and sit beside him.

Subhadda said to the Buddha: 'I have visited many spiritual teachers, and listened to their words with care, but I have never been sure whether their teaching is truly wise. So I have come to ask you: do these teachers possess the truth, or do they not?' The Buddha replied: 'There is a simple test as to whether a teacher is wise: if his teaching guides people onto the eightfold path, he is wise; if it does not guide people onto the eightfold path, he is not wise. I renounced the world at the age of twenty-nine, and decided to search for goodness and truth. I discovered the eightfold path, and have followed it for the past fifty-one years. Now I am on the point of entering nirvana.'

Maha Parinibbana Sutta 5.23–27

Last words

The Buddha said to Ananda: 'When I have died, the thought may arise in some people's minds: "Our teacher has died, so we can no longer be taught." Such a thought is quite wrong. Your teacher is not me personally, but the words I have uttered. Those words will be preserved long after my death. My teaching is the teacher.

'Until now all the monks have addressed one another as "friend". When I have died, I want you to change this. Senior monks may continue to call junior monks "friend", and they may add their family name. Junior monks should address senior monks as "sir", or "venerable sir".'

The Buddha then addressed the whole Community: 'It is possible that some doubt has arisen in your mind concerning some aspect of my teaching. Please feel free to raise any doubt now, so that I can answer it. I should prefer that you ask questions now, while we are still face to face, than that you reproach yourself after my death for not asking them.'

All the monks and nuns remained silent. The Buddha repeated himself, and again they remained silent. Ananda said: 'It is wonderful, lord, that in the entire Community there is not a single doubt or confusion.' The Buddha replied: 'Every member of this Community is in the stream that leads to the cessation of all suffering.'

Then he added: 'Decay is inherent in all creatures. Strive diligently!' These were his last words.

Maha Parinibbana Sutta 6.1–2, 5–7

Entering nirvana

The Buddha went into the first stage of meditation, and then quickly into the second and third stages. Finally he went into the fourth stage of meditation, after which he entered the sphere of the infinity of space.

He passed out of the sphere of the infinity of space, and into the sphere of the infinity of consciousness. And passing out of the sphere of the infinity of consciousness, he entered the sphere of nothingness. And passing out of the sphere of nothingness, he entered the sphere in which there is neither perception nor non-perception. And passing out of the sphere in which there is neither perception nor non-perception, he entered the sphere where all experience of perception ceases.

Ananda said to the monk Anuruddha: 'Our lord has entered nirvana.' Anuruddha replied: 'No, he has not yet entered nirvana. He is in the sphere where all experience of perception ceases.' Shortly afterwards the Buddha passed from the sphere where all experience of perception ceases, and entered nirvana.

Maha Parinibbana Sutta
6.8–9

THE DHAMMAPADA

The Dhammapada is without doubt the most famous part of the Pali Canon. It is a collection of aphorisms, which purport to be sayings of the Buddha himself; together they form a summary of the Buddha's moral and spiritual philosophy. Some have claimed that this collection was made at the first Council of the Buddha's monks, which convened within weeks of his death.

The chariot and the animal

From our past thoughts comes our present state of mind. From our present thoughts will come our future state of mind. Our life is the creation of our minds.

If we speak or act with an impure mind, suffering will follow – as surely as the chariot follows the animal that draws it.

If we speak or act with a pure mind, joy will follow – as surely as a shadow follows the person who casts it.

Some people look at others, and think: 'That person insulted me; that person upset me; that person defeated me; that person cheated me.' Their minds are never free from hate. Those who do not think such thoughts are free from hate.

Hate is never appeased by hate; it is appeased by love. This is an eternal law.

Most people do not bear in mind that one day all of us will die. But those who do bear this in mind settle their quarrels peacefully.

1–6

The monsoon wind

There are many who live only for pleasure, whose senses constantly seek new delights, who eat whatever they want, who are idle, and who do not distinguish between virtue and vice. The Devil shakes them, just as the monsoon wind shakes a weak tree.

There are some who do not live for pleasure, whose senses do not constantly seek new delights, who are careful in what they eat, who work hard, and who can distinguish clearly between virtue and vice. They cannot be shaken by the Devil, just as the monsoon wind cannot shake a mountain.

Those who put on the yellow robes of a monk, without learning self-control, and without purifying the soul of sensuous desires, are hypocrites. Those who acquire self-control, and whose souls are pure, can with honesty put on the yellow robes.

Those who think that which is unreal is real, and who think that which is real is unreal, are lost, and can never find the path to truth. Those who know what is real, and know what is unreal, are safely on the path to truth.

7–12

Thatch and rain

As the rain leaks into a house whose thatch is flimsy, passions leak into a mind whose self-discipline is poor. As a house with strong thatch keeps out the rain, a mind whose self-discipline is strong keeps out passions.

Those who do evil, will suffer in this life and the next. Evil itself will bring suffering to them; they will also be tortured with guilt when they reflect on what they have done. Those who do good, will be happy in this life and the next. Goodness itself will bring happiness to them; and they will be at peace with themselves when they reflect on what they have done.

The person who speaks holy words, but does not lead a holy life, is like a cowherd who counts his master's cattle. The person who speaks few holy words, but lives up to those words, is a true master.

13—20

The greatest treasure

Vigilance is the path to immortality; negligence is the path to death. Those who are vigilant never die; and those who are negligent are already dead.

The joy of vigilance consists in having a clear and wise mind which can see the truth; this is the joy which people of true holiness experience.

Those whose thoughts are high and whose meditation is deep, and who are walking along the Way, will ultimately attain nirvana, the incomparable bliss of perfect unity.

Those whose faith is strong, who always remember their high purpose, whose work is pure, whose actions are thoughtful, who are self-controlled, and who are always vigilant, will attain the supreme glory. They make an island for the soul, which no flood can overwhelm.

Those who are thoughtless in their actions, who do not seek to deepen their knowledge, and who are negligent, sink into spiritual oblivion.

Wise people regard watchfulness as the greatest treasure.

21–26

Thoroughbreds amongst carthorses

Never drop your guard of yourself; never surrender to pleasure and passion. Those who resist present pleasure will ultimately attain supreme joy.

Those who keep careful guard of themselves, break free from sorrow, and rise up the tower of wisdom; from the top they can look down on those still carrying the burden of misery. They see the suffering of the people of the world, as a mountaineer sees those in the valley below.

Those who are vigilant amongst the people of the world, are awake amongst sleepers; they are thoroughbreds amongst carthorses.

Those who are always vigilant, and never become negligent, are like fires; they burn all the obstacles in their path, both great and small.

Those who delight in vigilance, and who fear negligence, can never be defeated; they will win the ultimate victory of nirvana.

27–32

The straight shaft

The mind is unstable and unsteady; it is difficult to guard and control. Those who are wise straighten the mind, as the archer straightens the shaft of his arrows.

A fish, which has been caught and thrown on dry land, thrashes around; in the same way the mind struggles to free itself from the Devil.

The mind is fickle and flighty, wandering wherever it desires; it is difficult to restrain. Yet those who succeed in restraining their minds, experience great joy.

The mind is exceedingly subtle, and thus it is hard to comprehend. It flies in whatever direction it fancies. Yet those who succeed in understanding their minds, experience great joy.

The mind is mysterious, and it can move in many directions. Yet those who can attain mental harmony, break free from the shackles of the Devil.

Those whose minds are agitated, who do not know the path of truth, and whose faith is constantly wavering, shall never attain wisdom. But those whose minds are calm, who are free from passions and desires, and who have transcended good and evil, are wise and fearless.

33–39

The jar and the fortress

The body is fragile, like an earthen jar. So make your mind as strong as a fortress. Fight a constant battle against the Devil, who is constantly trying to tempt you. When you are victorious in a battle against the Devil, do not become complacent, but watch over your conquests. Always be vigilant.

Remember that before long your body will lie lifeless in the earth. It will be cast aside like a useless log of wood. Does that thought make you feel sad?

An enemy can hurt you; someone filled with hatred for you can harm you. But your mind, if it is wrongly directed, can do you far greater damage.

Your father or your mother or a relative can do you great good. But your mind, if it is rightly directed, can do you far greater good.

Who can gain victory over the world and the Devil? Who can overcome pain and death? Who can find the road of truth, the path of perfection – as a gardener can select the most beautiful flower?

The wise disciple gains victory over the world and the Devil. The wise disciple overcomes pain and death. The wise disciple finds the road of truth, the path of perfection – as a gardener selects the most beautiful flower.

The wise disciple knows that the body is the foam of a wave, the shadow of a mirage. The wise disciple breaks the sharp arrows of the Devil, which are concealed in the flowers of sensuous desires.

40–46

A heap of flowers

Those who gather the flowers of sensuous desires, are carried away — as a sleeping village may be carried away by a river breaking its banks.

The bee takes the nectar and flies away, without destroying the flower's beauty and fragrance. In the same way let people wander from place to place, taking the wisdom of the wise people they encounter.

Do not reflect on the sins of others, on the bad things they have done and the good things they have failed to do. Reflect only on your own sins, on the bad things you have done and the good things you have failed to do.

A blossom which is beautiful to the eye, but which has no fragrance, will never bear fruit. In the same way those who speak fine words, but do not act accordingly, will lead fruitless lives.

A blossom which is beautiful to the eye, and which has a rich fragrance, will bear abundant fruit. In the same way those who speak fine words, and live accordingly, will lead fruitful lives.

From a large heap of flowers many garlands and wreaths can be made. In the same way this life contains many opportunities to do good.

47–53

The scent of sandalwood

The fragrance of flowers does not travel against the wind; not even the scent of sandalwood, rose-bay or jasmine can defy the breeze which carries it. Yet the fragrance of virtue can travel against the wind; virtue can pervade the entire world with its pure scent.

Consider the scents of sandalwood, rose-bay, water lily and jasmine; they are exquisite. Yet the fragrance of virtue is supreme and unique in its beauty.

The fragrance of flowers, even that of rose-bay and sandalwood, cannot travel far. But the fragrance of virtue can travel higher than the highest cloud.

The path of those who are rich in virtue, who are constantly vigilant, and who are guided by the light of truth, cannot be crossed by the Devil. Such people are free from all wickedness.

A lily can grow and bloom on a heap of rubbish at the side of the road; its beauty can give joy to all who behold it, and its fragrance can inspire all who come near. In the same way people of great wisdom can rise up from the mass of ignorant humanity; their virtue can shine on all around them, and their words can uplift the souls of those who listen.

54–59

The long night

To those who cannot sleep, the night is long. To those who are weary, the road is long. To the fool who does not know the Way, the time between birth and death is long.

If on the great journey of life you cannot find a companion better than yourself, or at least as good, be happy to travel alone. Solitude is better than having a fool as a companion.

Fools are constantly anxious about their wealth, and they fret about their families. But they do not even own themselves, let alone their wealth and their families.

Fools who can recognize their own folly, are in this respect wise. But fools who think they are wise, are indeed real fools.

If a fool lives with someone who is wise, the fool never learns the path of wisdom, just as the spoon never learns the taste of the soup.

If an open-minded person encounters someone who is wise, even if their meeting lasts only a minute, the open-minded person will acquire wisdom – as the tongue enjoys the taste of the soup.

Fools who go through life thinking they are wise, are their own worst enemies. Their actions bear bitter fruit, which both they and others will be forced to eat.

60–66

Sour milk

If you act in such a way as to bring misery to others, do not pretend that your action was wise; instead, repent of that action, and make amends. If you act in such a way as to bring joy to others, do not criticize yourself; instead rejoice in your own wisdom.

Do not assume you have acted rightly until you see the fruits of your action. An action may at first seem good, but then later yield bitter fruit.

People may fast for many months, only consuming the tiniest quantities of food. Yet their efforts are worth nothing unless they feed their minds on the truth.

Just as it takes time for milk to turn sour, so it may take time for a wrong action to have evil consequences.

Ashes may conceal a smouldering fire. Smiles may conceal wickedness.

A fool may also be clever; but cleverness makes folly even more dangerous.

Some people yearn to be respected for their wisdom; they want to be venerated and given precedence over others. Such people are fools.

Some people yearn for others to be constantly seeking their advice; they love telling others what they should and should not do. Such people are puffed up with foolish pride.

You must choose between the path of material wealth, and that of nirvana.

Those who follow the Buddha do not strive for a high reputation, but strive only for salvation.

The carpenter and his timber

If someone reveals to you your faults, look upon that person as the guide to hidden treasure. Follow that person, knowing that you will discover the difference between good and evil.

Those who give wise instruction, showing people what is right and wrong, are loved by the wise and hated by fools.

Do not make friends with people whose souls are ugly, and who take delight in wickedness. Make friends only with people whose souls are beautiful, and who take delight in goodness.

Those who drink the waters of truth, have minds which are serene and restful. Those who love to hear the words of wise teachers, know that true joy consists in following the Way.

Those who dig ditches, control the flow of water. Those who make the shafts of arrows, control the direction of the arrows' flight. Carpenters control their timber. Similarly those who are wise, control their own minds.

Just as a great rock is not shaken by the wind, wise people are not shaken by praise or blame.

The soul of a person who has learnt the Way, is like a lake which is pure, peaceful and deep.

76–82

Pure light

Good people do not regard any object as a personal possession. Holy people do not desire any object. Good and holy
people transcend pleasure and pain, so their equanimity can
never be disturbed.

Do not crave for children, for power, or for wealth. Be indifferent to worldly success. Seek only virtue, righteousness
and wisdom.

Time is like a river, and most people run up the bank. To
reach nirvana you must cross the river to the other side.

Those who know and follow the Way, will cross the river
of time; and thus they will depart from the realm of death,
and enter eternity.

Leave the path of death, and follow the path of life. Leave
attachment to things and places, and instead enjoy the liberty
of detachment. Do not cling to foolish friends, instead rejoice
in solitude. Break free from possessions and from desires –
from whatever may darken the mind.

Attachment to things and to places is spiritual bondage,
and leads to darkness. Surrender all attachments, and enjoy
the pure light of spiritual freedom. Even in this mortal life
you can enjoy eternal nirvana.

83–89

The flight of birds

When spiritual travellers reach the end of their journey, they are released from all sorrows. The chains that bound them have dissolved; the burning passions which destroyed their happiness have been extinguished. They know the freedom of infinity.

Swans fly from their lake and rise in the air, searching for a better place to live. Similarly the thoughts of spiritual travellers rise up, seeking an eternal home.

Those who seek the food of life, reject excessive physical food; they want to be light enough to fly.

Spiritual travellers soar into the sky of liberation, into the infinite realm which has no beginning and no end. Their course is as mysterious as the flight of birds.

90–93

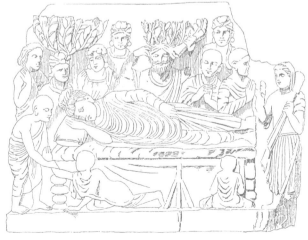

The enduring earth

Just as a good coachman controls his horses, so those who are wise control their senses. They do not surrender to any sensation which brings pleasure or inflames pride.

Those who are wise, are as enduring as the earth itself; they are as steady as a stone column; and they are as pure as a mountain lake. They are free from the cycle of death and rebirth – and they know they are free.

Those who have understood the Way, are at peace; their thoughts are peaceful, their words are peaceful, and their actions are peaceful.

Many people believe the most absurd religious doctrines; and by their incredulity they become spiritual slaves. Yet even the most sceptical people can believe in the nirvana, because it can be perceived directly; they can imagine for themselves the experience of being free from all temptation and desire.

Whether a holy person lives in a village or a forest, in a valley or on a hill, that place radiates joy. A holy person can make even the most remote and forbidding place beautiful and appealing. This is because the holy person's joy does not depend on the place, but is given to the place.

94–99

Two men

A single word that brings peace to the listener, is better than a thousand words which are empty of meaning.

A single verse that brings peace to the listener, is better than a thousand words which are empty of meaning.

A single poem that brings peace to the listener, is better than a thousand words which are empty of meaning.

Consider two men. One man is a great general, and conquers an empire. The other remains at home, and conquers himself. The latter has won the greater victory.

Consider two men. One visits the temple month after month, offering sacrifices to the gods. The other makes a single visit to someone who has conquered himself, and listens to his words. The latter has acted with greater wisdom.

Consider two men. One goes every day of his life to worship a sacred fire. The other pays reverence only once to someone who has conquered himself. The worship of the latter is more valuable.

Whatever acts of worship you perform in the course of a year, and whatever acts of charity you perform, they are worth nothing compared with listening and absorbing the teaching of those who are truly wise.

If you give honour to those who are rich in virtue and holiness, you will receive four treasures: long life, good health, spiritual strength, and eternal joy.

100–109

A single day

A single day devoted to virtue and contemplation, is better than a hundred years devoted to vice.

A single day passed in wisdom and vigilance, is better than a hundred years passed in ignorance.

A single day spent striving bravely for righteousness, is better than a hundred years spent in cowardly idleness.

A single day devoted to considering how things arise and cease, is better than a hundred years without considering how things arise and cease.

A single day perceiving the possibility of immortality, is better than hundred years lived in the shadow of death.

A single day following the Way, is better than a hundred years wandering without purpose.

110–115

Drops of water

Make haste in doing what is good, and keep your mind away from thoughts of evil. If you are slow in doing good, your mind will find pleasure in evil.

If you do evil, do not repeat your evil deed again and again. Beware of finding any pleasure in your sins; if your sins accumulate, they will become an intolerable burden.

If you do good, repeat your good deed again and again. Enjoy doing good; as your good deeds accumulate, they will make your heart light.

A person may find pleasure in evil deeds, so long as the evil has not yielded fruit. But when the fruit of evil ripens, the pleasure will turn to pain.

A person may find pain in good deeds, so long as the goodness has not yielded fruit. But when the fruit of goodness ripens, the pain will turn to pleasure.

Do not regard any sin as unimportant, saying to yourself it does not matter. Drops of water will eventually fill a jar; small sins can eventually fill you with sin.

Do not regard any good deed as unimportant, saying to yourself it does not matter. Drops of water will eventually fill a jar; small good deeds can eventually fill you with goodness.

116–122

Dust against the wind

A merchant with a precious load avoids the main roads, to keep safe from robbers. A person who loves life avoids drinking poison. In the same way you should avoid evil.

A man with no wound on his hand cannot be hurt by the poison he is carrying, since there is no place for the poison to enter his body. In the same way those with no evil cannot be hurt by evil.

If you do evil to someone who is good, to someone who is pure and free from sin, the evil will return to you like dust thrown against the wind.

All people are born on this earth. The wicked are reborn to a lower place. The righteous are reborn to a higher place. Those who are pure, attain nirvana.

You cannot escape the consequence of your evil actions by flying in the sky, nor by plunging to the depths of the ocean, nor by hiding in a mountain cave.

You cannot escape the power of death by flying in the sky, nor by plunging to the depths of the ocean, nor by hiding in a mountain cave.

123–128

A broken gong

All creatures tremble in the face of danger; all creatures fear death. When people reflect deeply on this, they no longer want to kill other creatures, or cause them to be killed.

Life is precious to all creatures. When people reflect deeply on this, they no longer want to kill other creatures, or cause them to be killed.

If for the sake of their happiness you refrain from harming other creatures, you yourself will find happiness.

Do not speak harsh words, because those who hear your words are liable to speak harshly in reply. Harsh words cause pain, and they may lead to physical blows.

A broken gong is silent. If you can attain utter silence, banishing all inner noise, you will have reached nirvana.

The farmer drives his cows each morning into the field. Old age drives all creatures into the field of death.

When people act with evil intent, they are lighting a fire in which one day they themselves will burn.

129–136

Whipping the horse

Many people deliberately hurt other creatures, even when those creatures are innocent and harmless. Such people will suffer at least one of these ills: chronic pain or infirmity; loss of limbs or terrible disease; madness or loss of mental faculties; persecution by the state authorities or false accusation; loss of possessions or loss of relations. And they will be reborn to a lower form of life.

Those whose spirits are defiled by doubt and desire, cannot be purified by ascetic practices – going naked, leaving the hair and the body unwashed, sleeping on the ground, covering the body with ashes, or constantly squatting.

Those whose spirits are pure and undefiled – who have no malice and are self-controlled, and who do not harm other creatures – cannot be corrupted by material luxury. They are true priests.

Is there a horse so noble that it is never whipped? Is there a person so noble as to avoid all blame?

Just as the whip drives the horse to gallop faster, let your faith drive you towards your goal of perfect holiness. Be energetic in your righteous actions and in your meditation; strive for virtue and wisdom. Then you will overcome all sorrow.

Those who dig ditches, control the flow of water. Those who make the shafts of arrows, control the direction of the arrows' flight. Carpenters control their timber. Similarly holy people control their own souls.

137–145

The frame and the plaster

How can people laugh and rejoice, when they are slaves to their own desires? Do they not realize that the darkness of ignorance envelops them? Will they not seek a lamp to enlighten them?

The body is like a puppet which is constantly liable to go wrong. Just as the puppet's paint may peel, the body's skin may develop rashes and ulcers. Just as the puppet's limbs may come loose, the body's bones may fracture and break. Just as the puppet will eventually wear out and be cast aside, so will the body.

The body is constantly decaying. It is a nest of diseases, a putrid heap of illnesses. It steadily disintegrates. All life ends in death.

Look at the white bones of a corpse whose flesh has withered away. Who can take pleasure in looking at them?

The body is like a house: the bones form the wooden frame, and the flesh is the plaster. Pride and hypocrisy dwell in this house. It will soon decay and collapse.

146–150

Even the glorious chariots of kings wear out; and so does the body. Yet the virtue of righteous people never grows old. To understand this truth is the beginning of enlightenment.

If people refuse to learn wisdom, they grow old like oxen: their bodies decay, and they possess no spiritual joy to balance the physical pain.

Through many lives I sought the one who built this house – who created the cycle of life and death – but did not find him. The awareness of suffering overwhelmed me.

Now I have seen the one who built this house; and having seen him, I can ensure the house is never built again. The rafters of sin are broken; the ridge-pole of ignorance is destroyed. All desire has been extinguished, and nirvana has been attained.

Those who do not learn self-control, who do not accumulate the riches of wisdom in their youth, will become like lanky herons standing beside a lake which has dried up in the summer heat.

Those who do not learn self-control, who do not accumulate the riches of wisdom in their youth, will become like broken bows – remembering glorious deeds of the past, which can never be repeated.

151–156

The diamond and the soft stone

If you respect yourself, you should watch over yourself with care. During the day and at night, throughout your life, be constantly vigilant.

Learn what is right, and establish in yourself the firm habit of always acting righteously. Then teach what you have learnt to others. In this way you will purify yourself.

If you practise what you believe, then you are worthy to teach others. Living up to your beliefs requires constant self-control.

No one can become your master; you alone are able to master yourself. When the master and the servant are the same, then there can be true service.

Do not blame others for the evil deeds that you do; blame only yourself. Only in this way will you avoid being crushed by your evil deeds − as a diamond can crush a soft stone.

157−161

The creeper and the tree

Just as a creeper can entangle a tree, so evil can entangle your soul. Just as a creeper can eventually pull a tree to the ground, so evil will pull your soul down to oblivion. Only your enemies will rejoice.

It is easy to do wrong; it is easy to betray your beliefs. It is hard to do right; it is hard to remain faithful to your beliefs. By doing wrong to others, you do wrong to yourself; by doing good to others, you do good to yourself.

Only fools scorn the teachings of those who are holy and righteous. They are gathering poisonous berries with which they will destroy themselves.

You alone can choose whether to do good or evil, whether to uplift or demean yourself, whether to purify or pollute yourself. No one can make this choice for you.

There are times when performing an evil act can seem righteous – because someone begs you to perform it, or because you believe it may lead to a greater good. Do not endanger your own soul in this way. Only perform actions which your soul approves.

162–166

A bubble of froth

Do not degrade yourself by the manner of your life. Do not be indolent. Beware of false teachings. Do not strive to prolong your life.

Awake! Watch yourself with care. Follow the Way. Those who follow the Way enjoy happiness in this life and the next.

Keep to the path of morality; avoid the path of immorality. Those who keep to the path of morality, enjoy happiness in this life and the next.

Look upon the world as a bubble of froth, as a mirage; then the king of death will have no power over you.

Consider the world: it is like a royal chariot painted in splendid colours. Fools yearn to sit in that chariot; but the wise are indifferent to it.

167–171

The moon on a cloudless night

A person who in earlier days was foolish, but has now acquired wisdom, is like the moon on a cloudless night, shedding a mysterious light across the world.

A person who in earlier days was evil, and is now good, is like the moon on a cloudless night, shedding a mysterious light across the world.

The world is indeed in darkness, and few can see the light. Just as few birds escape the hunter's net, only a few can fly freely to the light of wisdom.

Swans can follow the sun by flying. Human beings can avoid the forces of evil by flying above them.

Those who habitually tell lies, who hold morality in contempt, and who scorn the notion of rebirth – there is no evil to which such people may not sink.

Misers are not happy; fools do not praise generosity. But those who are generous with their wealth, enjoy happiness in this life and the next.

Imagine that you had power over the whole world; you would enjoy no rest, no peace.

There is a spiritual river which leads to nirvana. If you plunge into that river, you will enjoy eternal peace.

172–178

The net of poison

What earthly path could attract the Buddha? He wanders
freely through the pathless ways of infinite truth. His victory
over desire cannot be undone; he cannot be conquered.

What earthly path could attract the Buddha? He wanders
freely through the pathless ways of infinite truth. The net of
poisonous passions cannot capture him.

Even the highest angels yearn to be Buddhas. They long to
be fully alive and awake, to find peace in meditation, to be
peaceful and steady, to find joy in detachment.

To be born as a human being is hard; human beings are
constantly striving. Only a few hear and understand the Way;
only a few rise to become Buddhas.

Avoid evil, and do good. Keep your mind pure. This is the
teaching of all who are enlightened.

Abstaining from evil is the highest sacrifice. Nirvana is the
highest good. This is the teaching of all who are enlightened.

If you deliberately cause pain to another person, you cannot claim to be a follower of the Way. If you deliberately
offend another person, you cannot claim to be a follower of
the Way.

Not to hurt others by deeds or words; to acquire self-
control; to be moderate in eating; to sleep in solitude; to
meditate frequently – this is the teaching of all Buddhas.

179–185

A shower of gold coins

A shower of gold coins could not satisfy human desires. Besides, all pleasure leads to pain. So those who are wise do not seek pleasure. When desires depart, joy arrives; followers of the Buddha discover this truth.

People in fear of their lives flee to mountains or forests, or to sacred trees and shrines. But such places offer no refuge from suffering.

People in fear of spiritual destruction flee to the truth, and to Buddhas who are able to teach the truth. By this means they learn the four noble truths, concerning the existence of suffering, the origin of suffering, the cessation of suffering, and the path which leads to the cessation of suffering – the eightfold path.

The four noble truths are a safe refuge; they are the only refuge from suffering.

A person of true vision is hard to find; Buddhas are rare. Happy are those who know such a person.

Happy is the birth of a Buddha; happy is the teaching of the Way; happy is the harmony between those who follow the Way; happy are those who live in harmony.

Pay reverence to those worthy of reverence – to a Buddha or the disciples of a Buddha. Pay reverence to those who have abandoned evil, crossed the river of sorrow, and are free from fear. Pay reverence to those who know the glory of nirvana.

186–196

Living on bliss

Let us live joyfully. Let us form a community of love, in a
world full of hatred. Let us live without any kind of hatred.

Let us live joyfully. Let us form a community of spiritual
health, in a world full of illness. Let us live without any kind
of spiritual disease.

Let us live joyfully. Let us form a community of peace, in
a world full of rivalry. Let us live without any kind of rivalry.

Let us live joyfully. Let us form a community which pos-

sesses nothing. Let us live on spiritual
bliss, radiating spiritual light.

Victory of one person over another
brings hatred, because the defeated
person is filled with resentment. Those
who are indifferent to victory and defeat, find joy.

197–201

There is no fire like passionate desire. There is no evil like hatred. There is no pain like disharmony. There is no joy like nirvana.

Passionate desire is the greatest disease. Disharmony is the greatest sorrow. When you understand this, you know that nirvana is the greatest joy.

There is happiness in solitary silence. When you understand this, you are free from fear and sin, and you can feel the joy of the Way.

There is happiness in the company of people who are good. If the world had no fools, all would be happy.

There is sorrow in the company of fools, because to be with a person devoid of all wisdom is as painful as being with an enemy.

There is as much happiness in meeting a wise person, as in meeting a brother or sister who has returned from a long journey.

Make friends with people who are faithful, who are aware of the inner light, who are thoughtful and reflective, who are dutiful and noble. Just as the moon keeps company with the stars, so you should keep company with such friends.

202—208

Breaking the chains

Those who deliberately do what should not be done, and fail to do what should be done, forget their true purpose.

Those who indulge in transient pleasures, will eventually come to envy those who devote themselves to meditation.

Do not be attached to pleasure, and do not be anxious to avoid pain. If you remain attached to pleasure, its absence will cause you to suffer. If you are constantly anxious to avoid pain, its occurrence will cause you to suffer.

Those who are not attached to pleasure, and who are not anxious about pain, are free; they have broken the chains of suffering.

Attachment to pleasure produces fear and suffering; so those who are detached from pleasure, are also free from suffering and fear.

Passionate desire produces fear and suffering; so those in whom passionate desire has been extinguished, are also free from suffering and fear.

Sensuousness produces fear and suffering; so those who have learnt to control their senses, are also free from suffering and fear.

Desire produces fear and suffering; so those who desire nothing, are also free from suffering and fear.

209–216

Swimming upstream

Those who possess virtue and spiritual insight, who follow the Way that leads to perfection, who speak the truth, and who perform their duties with care, will win the affection of all good people.

Those who are determined to attain nirvana, and thus free themselves from all sensuous pleasures, are swimming upstream; they are going against the current of desire, in order to enjoy eternal bliss.

A man who has been away on a long journey, is welcomed with unrestrained joy on his safe return by his family and friends. You should regard your present life on earth as a long journey; and if you are to accomplish this journey safely, you must devote yourself to good works. Then when you are born into your next life, you will be welcomed by all around you; they will discern your natural virtue, and thus be delighted with you.

217–220

The good coachman

Forsake anger; renounce pride; detach yourself from all material possessions. No suffering can befall those who desire nothing.

Those who can control their anger are like good coachmen. When the carriage is at full speed, most coachmen merely hold the reins; but the good coachman still has perfect control of the horses.

Anger is conquered by love; evil is vanquished by goodness; meanness is overcome by generosity; lies are defeated by the truth.

Speak the truth; do not succumb to anger; give generously to those who ask – these three steps will put you on the path to perfection.

If you are wise, you will harm no living creature, and you will exercise perfect control over your body; then you will attain nirvana, where suffering is unknown.

If you are vigilant, you will watch over yourself day and night, and you will extinguish all passion; then you will attain nirvana, where suffering is unknown.

221–226

Solid gold

People criticize those who are silent; and they criticize those who speak at length; and they criticize those who speak only a little. No one can escape criticism in this world.

There never was, and there never will be, and there is not at present, a person who was universally criticized or universally praised.

But who would criticize the person who is praised by the wise, whose life is pure and radiant as solid gold, and who is virtuous and reflective? Even the Creator praises such a person.

Look out for any sign of anger in your actions, and suppress it. Control your actions so you do not hurt anyone, but only do good.

Look out for any sign of anger in your speech, and suppress it. Control your speech so you do not offend anyone, but only encourage them.

Look out for any sign of anger in your mind, and suppress it. Control your mind so you do not think ill of anyone, but only think well.

Those who can exercise perfect control of their actions, speech and mind, have acquired true wisdom.

227–234

Rusting iron

Your life is like a tree whose leaves have withered and turned brown. The messengers of death are approaching. You are on the point of departure. Have you made any provision for your journey?

Make a light for yourself; work quickly, and do not delay. Blow off the dust that weighs you down – the dust of sinful passion. Then your journey will take you to a new and glorious life.

Your life is coming to a close, and you are about to meet death. There is no resting-place on the road, and you have made no provision.

Make a light for yourself; work quickly, and do not delay. Blow off the dust that weighs you down – the dust of sinful passion. Then you will break free from the cycle of birth and death and rebirth; never again will you grow old.

Remove impurities from yourself, as a silversmith removes impurities from silver. Remove each impurity in turn, one by one.

If rust is allowed to develop on iron, and is not removed, eventually it will destroy the iron. Similarly if impurities are allowed to develop in the soul, and are not removed, the soul will be destroyed.

Dull repetition of sacred verses does nothing to remove rust on the soul.

Lack of exercise causes the body to rust, destroying its beauty. Lack of vigilance causes the soul to rust, destroying its beauty.

Uprooting and burning

A woman who commits adultery is condemned; yet a rich man who is mean with his wealth is equally sinful. Evil conduct causes suffering in this life and the next.

The root of sin is ignorance. Banish ignorance, and thereby you will rid yourself of sin.

Life seems easy for those who are shameless – who are boastful and aggressive, crafty and cunning, selfish and self-indulgent, arrogant and rude, corrupt and dishonest.

But life seems hard for those who strive for perfection – who are modest and peaceful, unselfish and unassertive, pure and radiant.

Those who destroy other living creatures, who tell lies, who take what is not given, who commit adultery, who frequently get drunk – they dig up the roots of life itself.

Be sure of this: lack of self-control leads to evil conduct. Be constantly vigilant, ensuring that greed does not undermine your hope of happiness.

Many people appear to be generous, but in fact are trying to gain advantage for themselves. Do not allow your mind to assess what people have given or not given. Making such judgements is incompatible with meditation.

Uproot all jealousy, and cast it on the fire. Then you can learn how to meditate.

242–250

The gambler

There is no fire like the fire of passion. There are no chains like the chains of hatred. There is no net like the net of illusion. There is no raging torrent like the raging torrent of desire.

It is easy to see the faults of others, but much harder to see your own faults. You can point out other people's faults as easily as pointing out chaff blowing in the wind. But you are liable to conceal your own faults as a cunning gambler conceals his dice.

If you only perceive and reflect upon other people's faults, and never perceive and reflect on your own, your own sins will steadily increase; and eventually they will become so great as to overwhelm you.

You cannot rise to holiness by soaring up into the sky; the path to holiness is within you. Pleasures are obstacles on the path.

To become enlightened you must cross the river of time. All material things pass away, but enlightenment lasts for all eternity.

251–255

Grey hairs

If you wish to follow the Way, do not use force to settle disputes. Instead calmly consider what is right and wrong, looking at all sides of the dispute. You should be concerned only with truth and peace. The truth is your guardian, and you are the guardian of the truth. In this way you will combine wisdom with virtue.

You do not demonstrate wisdom by constantly talking. Wisdom is demonstrated by serenity – by freedom from hate and fear.

You do not demonstrate wisdom by a display of fine scholarship. People do not need to be scholars in order to see and follow the right path; and those who follow the right path, may properly be called wise.

You do not demonstrate wisdom by having grey hairs on your head. If you have grown old without acquiring wisdom, you have passed your life in vain.

People may be regarded as elders if they are truly free from sin – if they are honest, virtuous, peaceful, self-controlled, and moderate.

Fine words and a graceful appearance are not worthy of honour, if behind the words and appearance lie envy, greed and deceit. Only if these three sins have been uprooted, and have been replaced by wisdom and love, should a person be treated with honour.

256–263

The warrior

A shaven head does not make a man a monk. A man with a shaven head is still capable of forgetting his vows, speaking dishonestly, and seeking wealth for himself. Anyone who makes peace out of conflict, whether the conflicts are great or small, is a true monk.

Begging for food does not make a man a monk. A man who begs for food is still capable of flouting the law of righteousness, and obeying the law of desire. Anyone who lives righteously, behaving with self-control and moderation, is a true monk.

Some people remain silent because their minds are empty; they are silent fools. Some people remain silent because they are weighing up carefully what is good and bad, in order to embrace what is good and reject what is bad; they are silent thinkers.

The warrior does not achieve greatness by killing other people. The true warrior fights against sin – and achieves greatness by not harming other living beings.

You cannot attain freedom by performing rituals, or by studying books, or by deep concentration, or by solitude.

Do not be self-satisfied. If you are self-satisfied, it is a sign that you have nothing to be satisfied about; the spiritual victory has not yet been won.

264–272

Removing thorns

The best of all paths is the eightfold path. The best of all truths are the four noble truths. The best of all spiritual states is freedom from desire. The best of all people are those who have become enlightened.

The eightfold path is the only path that leads to purity of vision. If you go on this path, you will confuse the Devil.

The eightfold path will take you to the cessation of all suffering; as you go along it, every thorn is removed from your soul. When I understood this, I decided to proclaim it to the world.

Great effort is required to move along the eightfold path; and you alone must make that effort. Great teachers can guide your steps, but you must take those steps. As you continue on the path, the chains of evil will fall from you.

All is transient. When you perceive this, you are above suffering; the path is clear.

All is suffering. When you perceive this, you are above suffering; the path is clear.

All is unreal. When you perceive this, you are above suffering; the path is clear.

273–279

Chopping down the forest

People should begin to strive for perfection when they are young. If young people lack spiritual determination, and thus sink into indolence, they will find it very difficult in later years to find the path of wisdom.

You should learn to control your speech, your thoughts and your actions, so that you never harm anyone. If your mouth, mind and body are pure, you will make spiritual progress.

Spiritual devotion brings light; lack of spiritual devotion brings darkness. Any sensible person will agree that light is preferable to darkness.

Desires are not the branches of a tree, but the trees of a forest. Your task is to cut down the entire forest and its undergrowth; then you will be free.

If even a single, small desire has not been chopped down, you are not free; you remain like a calf tethered to a cow.

280–284

The invincible king

Pluck out self-love, as you would pluck out a faded lotus at the end of summer. Then you can proceed along the eight-fold path which leads to peace – the perfect peace of nirvana, which has been expounded by all Buddhas.

The fool thinks: 'I can live in this place for ever, in winter and in summer, when it is raining and when it is dry.' But the fool does not consider death.

Even if you are perfectly satisfied with your lot – with your family and with your home – death will eventually carry you away, as a raging flood may carry away a sleeping village.

Neither parents nor children nor relatives can defeat the power of death. You should think of death as a king who can never be conquered; when he comes with his army, nothing can stop him.

Those who are wise and virtuous understand the power of death. That is why they strive to attain nirvana.

285–289

The multiple murderer

For every small pleasure that is forsaken, a greater spiritual joy is gained. And any sensible person will prefer the greater joy to the smaller pleasure.

Those who seek happiness for themselves by making others unhappy, are bound by the chains of hatred, and can never be free.

By not doing what should be done, and by doing what should not be done, sinful desires increase.

By taking care to do what should be done, and by taking care not to do what should not be done, sinful desires decrease.

Imagine that you had killed your father and mother, murdered two noble kings, and laid waste an entire country; you could still be purified. No sin is so great that a person cannot be purified of it.

Imagine that you had murdered several Buddhas; you could still be purified. No sin is so great that a person cannot be purified of it.

290–295

The followers of Gautama Buddha are awake and constantly vigilant; by night and by day they remember the teachings of their master.

The followers of Gautama Buddha are awake and constantly vigilant; by night and by day they remember the Way which he teaches.

The followers of Gautama Buddha are awake and constantly vigilant; by night and by day they remember their holy Community.

The followers of Gautama Buddha are awake and constantly vigilant; by night and by day they remember the transitory nature of the body.

The followers of Gautama Buddha are awake and constantly vigilant; by night and by day they find joy in loving all living beings.

The followers of Gautama Buddha are awake and constantly vigilant; by night and by day they find joy in profound meditation.

296–301

The edge of the forest

It is hard and painful to renounce the pleasures of the world. It is hard and painful to remain in the world, and yet not enjoy its pleasures. It is hard and painful to follow the Way as a monk, and equally hard and painful to follow the Way as a householder. It is hard to live amongst people who do not agree with your beliefs.

Remaining trapped in the cycle of birth and death is more painful than following the Way. Travelling on the unending road of birth and death is far worse than travelling on the road leading to nirvana. So leave the road of birth and death, and take the road to nirvana.

Those who possess spiritual devotion and virtue, possess the most precious of all treasures; and such people are revered wherever they go.

The snowy peaks of the Himalayas can be seen far and wide. In the same way people who possess virtue and wisdom become known far and wide.

Remove yourself from the forest of desires; live and sleep alone on the edge of the forest. There you will find true joy.

302–305

Those who utter falsehoods to others, condemn themselves. Those who commit an evil deed, and then deny that they committed it, doubly condemn themselves. They will suffer both in this life and the next.

Many people wearing the yellow robes of a monk are not pure, because they have not learnt self-control. Their hypocrisy condemns them.

It would be better for a false monk to swallow a ball of red-hot iron, than to eat the food given to him by good people.

When people commit adultery, they suffer four consequences: they degrade themselves; they cannot sleep easily; they earn the contempt of others; and they are reborn at a lower level.

The pleasures of adultery are fleeting, but the bitter consequences last long. So only the most ignorant fool commits adultery.

A blade of sharp grass, when wrongly handled, lacerates the skin. In the same way asceticism, when wrongly practised, lacerates the soul.

An act of devotion carelessly performed, a religious rite improperly observed, a sacred vow broken – all these produce sour fruit. You should do everything to the best of your ability.

A thoughtless pilgrim raises dust walking along the road – the dust of indolence and passionate desires.

306–313

A frontier town

It is better to do nothing, than to do something wrong; doing wrong produces a raging fire of suffering. It is better to do what is right, than to do nothing; doing right extinguishes the fire of suffering.

A frontier town is guarded well, both from outside invasion and internal subversion. Guard yourself with equal care.

Do not drop your guard for a moment − because at the moment your guard is dropped, the Devil will seize his chance, and you will be condemned to great suffering.

Some people feel guilty when there is no reason for guilt. Others do not feel guilty even when there is ample reason. Ensure that your feelings of guilt are properly matched to your behaviour.

Some people feel fear when there is no reason for fear. Others do not feel fear even when there is ample reason. Ensure that your feelings of fear are properly matched to your situation.

Those who can distinguish clearly between right and wrong, between good and evil, and can match their emotions to what they perceive, will always do what is right and good.

314−319

The elephant in battle

Just as in battle the elephant quietly endures the arrows shot from the bow, so I shall silently endure abusive words that are hurled at me.

Elephants are trained to carry warriors into battle, and to carry kings in triumphal processions. We should train ourselves to withstand insults, so that we remain calm and serene.

Mules and horses and elephants have to be trained by people. But people must train themselves.

An animal cannot carry you to the land of spiritual bliss – to nirvana. You must carry yourself.

In captivity elephants are liable to become weak and indolent; they dream of the forest which is their natural home. And pigs who are kept in sties become lazy and sleepy. Most human beings are held captive by their passionate desires; they are tethered to the wheel of death and rebirth.

In the past my mind used to stray wherever selfish desire would lead it. Today it does not stray. It is peaceful because I have learnt to control it, just as the trainer controls the elephant.

Be vigilant; keep watch over your thoughts. Pull yourself up from the mire of sinful thoughts, as the elephant pulls himself out of a swamp.

320–327

Sweetness

On the journey of life seek a wise friend, who is virtuous and
diligent. Then with joy and with vigilance you will together
overcome the obstacles on the road.

But if you cannot find a wise, virtuous and diligent friend,
travel alone – like a king exiled from his own country, or a
solitary elephant in the forest.

It is better to travel alone on the journey of life, than to
have a fool for a companion. Leave behind your desires, your
passions and your sins, and become like the solitary elephant
in the forest.

It is sweet to have a friend in need. It is sweet to share
enjoyments with a friend. It is sweet to have done some good
in this life. It is sweet to cast aside all pain.

It is sweet to be a mother. It is sweet to be a father. It is
sweet to be a monk. It is sweet to be a saintly priest.

It is sweet to be virtuous throughout life. It is sweet to
have faith which is pure and strong. It is sweet to attain wisdom. It is sweet to be free from sin.

328–333

Creepers and waves

If you are not striving for nirvana, your desires will grow like a creeper. You will jump from death to death – like a monkey jumping from tree to tree in a forest, yet finding fruit on none of them.

Just as a creeper can entangle and eventually destroy a tree, so your desires will entangle and destroy your soul.

But if you can overcome your desires, then suffering will slip away from you, like drops of water slipping off the lotus flower.

Therefore in a spirit of love I tell you: cut from your soul the creeper of desire.

Do not let the Devil push you down, as the current of the river pushes down the reeds near the bank.

A tree which has been chopped down can grow again, so long as the roots are not damaged. In the same way passionate desires can grow again, so long as their roots remain in place.

When the waves of desire continue to flow towards pleasure, the soul will be carried away.

Waves of desire flow everywhere, carrying souls away; creepers of desire grow everywhere, entangling souls. Stop the flow and uproot the creepers, using the power of wisdom.

334–340

The spider in its web

If youth is devoted to pleasure, old age is beset by pain.

People who are pursued by desire, run round like hunted hares. To conquer desire, you must first turn away from its objects.

Those who are free from desire, find joy in solitude. But such people may at any time return to old desires. Then others will say: 'They were free, but ran back to their prison.'

Fetters made of iron, wood or rope are as nothing compared with the fetter of desire.

The fetter of desire – for gold and jewels, for a wife and sons – is exceedingly strong. It may seem soft, but it drags down the soul, and is hard to undo. Thus it is better to cut the fetter by renouncing pleasure and walking away from worldly concerns.

Sometimes a spider becomes entangled in its own web. In the same way human beings create desires, in which their own souls become entangled. Thus it is better to cut the web of desire by renouncing pleasure and walking away from worldly concerns.

Leave the past behind; leave the future behind; leave the present behind. You are then ready to go to the other shore – never to return to a life which ends in death.

341–348

The end of the journey

If you allow yourself to be disturbed by wrong thoughts, if you do not control your passions, and if you indulge yourself in sensuous pleasures, then the chains of desire binding your soul will grow stronger.

But if you pacify your thoughts, if you reflect on the suffering which pleasure causes, and if you meditate on the light within you, then the chains of desire will weaken and break.

When you reach the end of your spiritual journey, your mind will be serene; the thorns of suffering will have been burnt away, and you will enjoy perfect peace.

Those who are free from lust and greed and every other kind of desire, are able to think clearly. They can understand the meaning of words and phrases, because they can discern the inner meaning of all things.

I have conquered all. I know all truth, because my life is pure. I have renounced all pleasure, so I am free from desire. I know the Way. Who can be my teacher? Whom shall I teach?

349–353

Weeds

The gift of truth is more precious than all other gifts. The taste of truth is sweeter than all other tastes. The joy of truth surpasses all other joys. The loss of desires conquers all suffering.

Greed is a deadly enemy; all who succumb to greed, are destroyed by it.

Weeds harm crops, and passions harm the soul. Gifts offered to those free from passions bring a great reward.

Weeds harm crops, and hate harms the soul. Gifts offered to those free from hate bring a great reward.

Weeds harm crops, and illusions harm the soul. Gifts offered to those free from illusions bring a great reward.

Weeds harm crops, and desires harm the soul. Gifts offered to those free from desires bring a great reward.

354–359

Exercising control

Controlling the eye is good. Controlling the ear is good. Controlling the sense of smell is good. Controlling the sense of taste is good.

Controlling the body is good. Controlling speech is good. Controlling the mind is good. Controlling the inner spirit is good. When you have achieved perfect self-control, you leave all suffering behind.

Controlling the hands is good. Controlling the feet is good. Controlling the tongue is good. Controlling the emotions is good. When you have achieved perfect self-control, you find inner joy and peace. You are a true monk.

Listen to those who are self-controlled, peaceful, wise and humble. Their words are sweet. They can throw light on the inner meaning of ancient religious verses.

Remain firmly on the Way. Find joy in following the Way. Meditate on the Way. Constantly ponder on the Way. Then you will never go astray.

360–364

A ship with no cargo

The monk should never despise what has been given to him.
Nor should he be jealous of what has been given to others;
jealousy destroys meditation.

Even if the monk is given very little to eat on a particular
day, he should not despise the morsels he has received.
Gratitude for every gift purifies the spirit, and earns the respect of others.

The monk should not regard anything as his own. He
should not wish to possess anything for himself. And he
should not allow his imagination to dwell on comforts and
pleasures he should not enjoy.

The soul of the monk should be filled with love, and his
mind should be filled with the teachings of the Buddha. Then
he will follow the Way that leads to nirvana – to the realm
where suffering has been banished and joy is supreme.

A ship with no cargo sails faster than a ship laden with a
heavy cargo. Empty yourself of the cargo of passions and desire; then you will sail swiftly towards the land of nirvana.

Cut off the five chains of selfishness, doubt, excessive austerities, lust and hate. Throw off the five chains of desire,
passion, self-will, restlessness and ignorance. Instead cherish
faith, vigilance, energy, meditation and vision. When the
chains have fallen from your soul, you will sail safely to the
other shore.

365–370

An empty house

Be vigilant. Be ambitious in your meditation. Do not think about pleasure, and then you will not need to think about pain. Thinking about pleasure is like swallowing a red-hot ball of iron.

If you lack wisdom, you will not meditate; if you do not meditate, you will not acquire wisdom. Wisdom and meditation will carry you towards nirvana.

A peaceful mind is like an empty house. As you enter an empty house, you find silence and stillness. You enter your own mind through meditation; and if your mind is at peace, you will find silence and stillness.

A peaceful mind is lit by the light of truth. When you can see this light clearly within your own mind, you experience the perfect and eternal bliss of nirvana.

If you wish to tread the path leading to nirvana, you must first learn to control your senses and to behave according to the highest standards of morality. Make friends with people who also wish to tread this path, so that you can encourage each other.

Let love guide your actions. Perform your duties to the best of your abilities. Then you will start to tread the path which leads away from suffering towards perfect joy.

371–379

The full moon on a clear night

Just as the jasmine sheds its withered leaves, you should shed
every type of malice and wickedness.

Let your actions, speech and thoughts always be peaceful.
Become the master of yourself. Cast aside all bodily desires.

Arise! Wake up to the call of your own soul. Train yourself to obey your own soul. Take shelter under your own
soul. Watch over your own soul. Be sure that the soul is the
source of all joy.

As a merchant trains his horse, you should train yourself.
Become the master of yourself.

Time passes quickly, but the teaching of the Buddha
lasts for all time. Pleasures pass quickly; but the teaching of
the Buddha leads to joy which transcends time – the joy of
nirvana.

A young person can follow the Buddha's teaching as well
as an old person. The teaching of the Buddha is like the full
moon on a clear night; it shines in the darkness, shedding its
light everywhere.

380–382

Light on the warrior's armour

Cross over the stream of desire. Do not let the torrent of passions carry you away. On the far bank of the stream is the realm of bliss.

In the realm of bliss there is perfect serenity. Knowledge of all kinds is redundant; the truth is perfectly manifest.

In the realm of bliss fear is absent. The senses are redundant, and so is thought.

In the realm of bliss meditation is perfectly pure and peaceful. There is no passion to disturb the tranquillity. No further effort is required, because the final destination has been reached.

By day the sun shines, and by night the moon shines; their light glints on the warrior's armour. The teaching of the Buddha shines by day and by night; and its light glints on the souls of those who are truly awake.

Those who have discarded evil, are true monks. Those who live in peace with others, are true priests. Those who rid themselves of all impurities – greed, hate, delusion, pride, speculation, doubt, torpor, restlessness, lust and hardness of heart – are true hermits.

383–388

Tangled hair

Do not return evil for evil. Your birth does not determine your status; this is determined by your capacity to endure evil without retaliation.

Renounce all worldly attachments. Your birth does not determine your status; this is determined by your capacity for detachment.

Do not think, speak or act with malice. Your birth does not determine your status; this is determined by your capacity to suppress malice within you.

Find a teacher who teaches what the Buddha taught. Revere your teacher, as a priest reveres the sacrificial fire.

Your clothes or the length of your hair or your birth do not determine whether you are holy. The strength of your commitment to the truth determines whether you are holy.

Tangled hair or rough leather garments are no proof of holiness. You must untangle your passions, and brush every kind of desire from your soul.

Do not be anxious about what you wear and what you eat. Go into the forest, and learn to meditate.

389–395

Water on the lotus leaf

If you were born into a family of priests, do not be spiritually proud. It is not birth, but the attainment of self-control, that makes a person holy.

If you were born into a wealthy family, do not regard that wealth as an advantage to you. In order to become holy, you must free yourself from all possessions.

If you wish to be holy, you must cut the chains of attachment, and become perfectly free.

Cut the strap of ill will, the thong of desire, the chain of doubt, and the crossbar of ignorance; then you will be holy.

Imagine that you are accused of crimes you did not commit, and you are flogged and imprisoned for those crimes. If you can endure such an unjust punishment without bitterness or resentment, then you are truly holy.

If you are free from anger and from lust, and if you are perfectly virtuous and self-controlled, then your present body will be your last; you are truly holy.

If you do not cling to sensuous pleasures, just as water does not cling to the leaf of the lotus, or a grain of mustard does not cling to the point of a needle, then you are truly holy.

If you know that there is no escape from suffering in this world, and therefore you wish to lay down the burden of earthly life, then you are truly holy.

396–402

Mustard seed on a needle

If your vision is profound and wise, if you can distinguish clearly right from wrong, and if you always walk on the path of righteousness, then eventually you will attain true holiness.

If you are indifferent as to whether you have a home or are a homeless wanderer, you are truly holy.

If you do not hurt any living creature, whether it be strong or weak, and if you do not cause others to hurt or kill any living creature, you are truly holy.

If you are tolerant towards the intolerant, if you are peaceful towards the violent, if you are generous towards the greedy, you are truly holy.

If you fall away from lust, hate, pride and dishonesty, as a mustard seed falls from the point of a needle, you are truly holy.

If your speech is always peaceful, useful and sincere, causing offence to no one, you are truly holy.

If you never take anything that has not been given to you – be it long or short, large or small, good or bad – you are truly holy.

403–409

The muddy river

If your body is free from desire, and thus you enjoy the infinite freedom of detachment, you are truly holy.

If your mind is free from doubt, and thus you enjoy the infinite freedom of faith, you are truly holy.

If you have transcended good and evil, and thus you enjoy the infinite freedom of perfect love, you are truly holy.

If you take no pleasure in fleeting, transient things, and thus your soul is as pure, bright, clear and serene as the moon, you are truly holy.

If through meditation you have crossed the muddy river that divides the world of death and rebirth from the realm of nirvana, and are thus free from all doubts and desires, you are truly holy.

If you abandon your home, leaving behind you all material attachments, you are truly holy. But be vigilant, lest material attachments catch you up.

If you abandon your home, leaving behind you all worldly ambition, you are truly holy. But be vigilant, lest worldly ambition catches you up.

If you have no material or moral debts to other people, and can wander freely without anxiety, you are truly holy.

410–417

The river ceasing to flow

If you are free from pleasure and pain, if you are inwardly serene, and if the seeds of death and rebirth have been burnt within your soul, you are truly holy.

If you are a spiritual hero, bravely fighting and conquering all evil passions, you are truly holy.

If the cycle of death and rebirth is over, and you have joyfully reached your final destination, you are truly holy.

If your soul is fully awake, and can see the fullness of truth, you are truly holy.

If you are following the hidden path to perfection, which men and women of the world cannot see, you are truly holy.

If you are indifferent to the future, the past, and the present, you are truly holy.

If you possess nothing and desire nothing, you are truly holy.

If you have become the king of yourself, the supreme monarch of your own soul, you are truly holy.

If you can see yourself as you really are, and can thus rid yourself of all impurities, you are truly holy.

Your past lives are like a great river which has flowed for thousands of years in every part of the world. If that river has ceased to flow, you are truly holy.

418–423

MAHAYANA WISDOM

The earliest Buddhist missions outside India were to Sri Lanka and Burma in the third century BCE; and Buddhism gradually spread through much of south-eastern Asia. The Buddhists here tended to regard only the Pali Canon as authoritative. Buddhism also spread northwards, reaching China by at least the first century CE; and from the fifth century CE it was adopted in Tibet. Already in India some Buddhist groups had been developing doctrines and spiritual techniques that went beyond the Buddha's teachings; and in China and Tibet this development continued. These newer forms of Buddhism called themselves Mahayana, meaning 'great vehicle', distinguishing themselves from the older Hinayana, meaning 'small vehicle'.

The three most famous works in Mahayana are the *Diamond Sutra*, the *Heart Sutra*, and the *Lotus Sutra*, each of which is frequently referred to by later writers. They were all composed in India, but were translated into Chinese, and were widely regarded in China as scriptural. None has a single author, but they each developed over two or three centuries, appearing in their present forms by the fourth century CE.

Two further works composed in India have played a central part in Mahayana Buddhism. The *Lankavatara Sutra* appeared early in the fifth century, and is widely regarded as containing the essence of Mahayana wisdom. One of the first Buddhist works to whom an author can be attached, is the *Bodhicaryavatara*, written by Shantideva, a monk in north India, in the eighth century. Like the *Dhammapada*, it takes the form of a series of aphorisms. Shantideva's monastery was visited by monks from both China and Tibet, and his book circulated widely in both countries.

One of the earliest Buddhist works composed in China itself was the *Surangama Sutra*, a shapeless work which contains within it some spiritual gems; it is manifestly a compilation of the work of different writers.

The greatest figure in Tibetan Buddhism was Milarepa, who lived in the eleventh century CE. He composed a series of poems and meditations, which indirectly tell the story of his life, first as a seeker, and then as a teacher. One of Milarepa's disciples, Dvagpo-Lharje, sought to encapsulate all spiritual wisdom in a series of simple precepts.

Enlightened men and women

Enlightened men and women must lead to nirvana all living beings in the universe: those who are born from an egg; those who are born from a womb; those who are born within water; those who are born by transformation; those who are born with form, and those who are born without form; those who are born with perception, and those who are born without perception; and those who are born with neither perception nor non-perception. Enlightened men and women must lead all these into the realm of nirvana where there is perfect freedom.

Innumerable beings have been led to nirvana by enlightened men and women; yet no being at all has been led to nirvana. How is this? If enlightened people conceive the notion of being, they are not enlightened. An enlightened man or woman has no notion of self or being, no notion of a mind or a person.

Vajracchedika Prajnaparamita Sutra (Diamond Sutra) 3

Detached love

Enlightened men and women should practise love; and yet
their love should be detached. This means they should practise love without regard to appearances – without regard to
sound, odour, taste, or any other attribute. Their love should
not be motivated by attachment, nor lead to attachment. The
merit that accrues from detached love is beyond measure.

Can you measure all the space to the east? Can you measure all the space to the south, west or north? Can you
measure all the space downwards or upwards? Equally incal-
culable is the merit gained by enlightened men and women
who practise love without regard to appearances.

Vajracchedika Prajnaparamita Sutra (Diamond Sutra) 4

Filled with faith

An enlightened man or woman cannot be recognized by any material feature. This is because material features are not in reality material features. Material features are delusions; and those who perceive that material features are not material features, perceive the nature of enlightenment.

Many centuries after the passing of Gautama Buddha, there will be people of great self-control, who will hear the true teaching and believe in it. This is because they will already have acquired great merit. But you should realize that they have acquired this merit not just under one enlightened teacher, nor two enlightened teachers, nor three, four or five enlightened teachers, but under countless enlightened teachers; so their merit is of every kind. These people, as soon as they hear the true teaching, will be filled with faith. They will no longer cherish the ego; they will no longer see themselves as distinct and separate individuals. Indeed, if they saw any person or object as distinct and separate, they would still be clinging to the notion of ego.

Ultimately true teaching must itself be relinquished; but false teaching must be relinquished first.

Vajracchedika Prajnaparamita Sutra (Diamond Sutra) 5, 6

Teaching the truth to others

Let us imagine that someone filled the three thousand worlds
in the universe with treasure – with gold, silver, lapis lazuli,
crystal, agate and pearls – and then gave that treasure to the
poor. That person would gain great merit. Let us imagine that
someone heard and understood four lines of true teaching,
and then explained those lines to others. That person would
gain even greater merit.

Let us imagine there were as many rivers as there are
grains of sand in the bed of one river; the number of grains
of sand in the beds of all the rivers would be beyond calcu-
lation. If someone gave away seven treasures for every grain
of sand in the bed of all those rivers, that person would gain
great merit. But if someone heard and understood four lines
of true teaching, and then explained those lines to others, that
person would gain even greater merit.

Vajracchedika Prajnaparamita Sutra (Diamond Sutra) 8, 11

Perfect forbearance

Enlightened men and women demonstrate perfect forbearance. A king may cut flesh from every limb of an enlightened person; yet the enlightened person will show no response. But this perfect forbearance is not perfection. Why? An enlightened person has no perception of self; and as a consequence an enlightened person cannot conceive of ill-will against the self. This loss of all perception of self, and all conception of ill-will against the self, is the consequence of five hundred previous lives, devoted to acquiring forbearance.

Enlightened men and women, having lost all perception of self, should raise their souls to the highest, best and most perfect enlightenment. They should have thoughts which have no images, no visions, no sounds, no smells, and no feelings; their thoughts should have no objects. Their thoughts should not even concern the Way, or the absence of the Way; their thoughts should have no concerns.

Vajracchedika Prajnaparamita Sutra (Diamond Sutra) 14

Liberating all living beings

Enlightened men and women should be resolved to save all
living beings. But they should know that when all beings
have been saved, in truth no being has been saved. This is
because the notion of liberating a living being assumes that
living beings exist as separate, distinct entities, each with its
own ego; yet salvation leads to the understanding that there
are no separate, distinct entities, and therefore no egos.

There is no formula for attaining enlightenment. Enlightenment is attained by going beyond all the realm of formulations; enlightenment is neither real nor unreal.

Imagine enlightened people saying: 'I shall save all living creatures.' In saying those words they would reveal that
they are not truly enlightened. An individual person cannot
be enlightened, because enlightenment involves the annihilation of the notion of individuality. Truly enlightened people
are devoid of any idea of separate selfhood.

Vajracchedika Prajnaparamita Sutra (Diamond Sutra) 17

Truth beyond teaching

Do not imagine that an enlightened teacher ever intends to teach the truth. Anyone who says that enlightened teachers intend to teach the truth, is insulting enlightenment, and does not understand true teaching. Truth cannot be put into words; therefore it cannot be taught.

In attaining enlightenment, nothing is gained; there is no profit whatever from attaining enlightenment. Enlightenment is attained through breaking free from all sense of self, and through cultivating every kind of goodness.

Do not imagine that an enlightened teacher ever cherishes the idea of liberating all living beings. In reality there are no living beings. If a teacher believed there were living beings to be saved, that teacher would still be entangled in ideas of the self, the personality, the ego, and separate individuality.

Vajracchedika Prajnaparamita Sutra (Diamond Sutra) 21, 22, 23, 25

Foolish thoughts about enlightenment

Some people imagine that enlightened teachers have the marks of great imperial rulers. Some imagine that enlightened teachers can be recognized by their outward appearance. And some imagine that enlightened teachers can be recognized by the quality of their voice. But those who think that enlightened teachers have some distinguishing features, have not understood the nature of enlightenment; their footsteps are straying from the path of truth.

Some people imagine that people attain enlightenment by virtue of the perfection of their form. Others imagine that on attaining enlightenment people are no longer visible or audible. Such thoughts are foolish, and should not be entertained.

Vajracchedika Prajnaparamita Sutra (Diamond Sutra) 26, 27

Bubbles in a stream

Imagine that an enlightened man or women gave to the poor as many treasures as there are grains of sand in the bed of a river. And imagine that another enlightened man or woman realized that all living beings are devoid of ego; and in the light of this realization attained perfect wisdom. The merit of the latter would far exceed the merit of the former. Yet all truly enlightened people are indifferent to merit, because they have no desire for rewards.

Imagine that a group of people took all the worlds in the universe, and ground them to dust. The number of grains of dust would be beyond counting. Yet even if that group analyzed every single grain, they would not understand the nature of the universe. Only ignorant people could think that such an analysis would be fruitful.

People can only understand reality by detaching truth from appearances. They must learn to think of appearances as bubbles in a stream, and as flashes of lightning in a storm — which pass away in an instant. They must think of this world as a flickering lamp, a phantom, and a dream.

Vajracchedika Prajnaparamita Sutra (Diamond Sutra) 28, 30, 32

Form and lack of form

Homage to perfect wisdom; homage to that which is beautiful and holy.

An enlightened man called Avalokita, a holy master, was swimming in the deep river of wisdom – the wisdom that goes beyond all wisdom. Then he looked down, and saw five mounds; and he realized that in themselves they had no form.

Avalokita said to his disciple: 'Form has no form, and lack of form is form. Lack of form is not different from form; and form is not different from lack of form. That which has form, has no form; that which has no form, has form. The same is true of emotions, perceptions, sensations and thoughts.'

Then Avalokita said to his disciple: 'All spiritual ways lack form; that is what makes them distinct. Spiritual ways are not constructed by anyone; they do not start or finish anywhere; they are neither pure nor polluted; they are neither incomplete nor complete.'

Prajnaparamita Hridaya Sutra (Heart Sutra) 1–4

Spiritual ways

Avalokita, an enlightened man, said to his disciple: 'On all spiritual ways there is no form, no emotion, no perception, no sensation, and no thought. There is no eye, ear, nose, tongue, body or mind. There are no colours, sounds, smells, tastes or textures. The consciousness is not conscious or unconscious. There is neither ignorance nor knowledge. There is neither decay nor death; and there is neither lack of decay nor lack of death. There is no suffering; there is no starting nor stopping. Indeed, on all spiritual ways there is no way. There is no rationality, no progress, and no lack of progress.'

Avalokita continued: 'Enlightened men and women are indifferent to any kind of personal attainment. They do not wish to justify themselves. They put their trust in perfect wisdom. In their indifference to personal attainment, and their lack of desire for self-justification, enlightened men and women can never be humiliated or upset by others. Ultimately they attain nirvana.'

Prajnaparamita Hridaya Sutra (Heart Sutra) 5–6

Father and children in a burning house

There was a man who was rich beyond measure. His house was vast, but had only one door. One day a fire broke out in the house, and quickly spread through its rooms. The man had many children – twenty, thirty, or even forty – who were playing in one of the rooms. They were quite unaware of the fire.

The man ran to the room where the children were playing, told them about the fire, and urged them to leave at once. But they were so engrossed in their games that they did not listen to him. He told them that, unless they left quickly, they would be burned to death by the fire. This time they listened to him; but since they did not understand what a fire was, they did not take him seriously.

Then the father said: 'In the garden outside the house there are many new toys, which are rare and hard to find. For example, there are toy carts on which you can ride. I suggest you go and play with these new toys.' The children were excited by the prospect of having new toys; so they ran out of the house, and their lives were saved.

In this parable the father represents an enlightened teacher, and the children represent ordinary human beings.

Saddharma Pundarika (Lotus Sutra) 3

The father, the son and the workers

There was a man who was rich beyond measure, with a great estate and many workers. He had a son, who ran away from home. The son took various menial jobs, and was reduced to poverty. The father searched everywhere for his son, but could not find him.

After many years the son had forgotten where his father lived; and, without realizing what he was doing, returned to his father's house, and asked for work. The father recognized his son at once. But the father knew that, if he revealed himself immediately, that son would be frightened and humiliated, and run away. So the father instructed his steward to give his son the task of cleaning the latrines.

When the son had been cleaning the latrines for a few days, the father smeared himself with dirt, put on rough clothes, and joined the son in this task. The son did not recognize his father; but gradually he learned to trust his father as a friend. Eventually, when they had been working together for many months, the father told his son who he was. The son burst into tears, and embraced his father – and, through his tears, apologized for having run away.

The father taught his son how to run the estate, and how to care for the workers. Then the father died, and the son took over.

In this parable the father is an enlightened teacher, the son is his successor, and the workers are the men and women whom they guide.

Saddharma Pundarika (Lotus Sutra) 4

The thick forest

There is a large, thick forest. It has plants and trees of every size and hue. There are streams running through it, and there are many different kinds of soil within it. Amidst the plants and trees there are medicinal herbs, whose fragrance spreads throughout the forest. A dense cloud hovers over the forest, and moistens all the trees, plants and medicinal herbs, so that they can grow and thrive.

In this parable the trees and plants represent the many different types of people that inhabit the earth. The different types of soil represent the different nations and cultures in which people live. The medicinal herbs are the enlightened teachers. And the dense cloud is the truth.

Saddharma Pundarika (Lotus Sutra) 5

Perfect intelligence and compassion

If you survey the world with perfect intelligence and compassion, it seems like a flower, which blossoms briefly, and quickly dies. The terms 'being' and 'non-being' cannot be applied to it.

If you survey the world with perfect intelligence and compassion, it seems like a dream; it appears, and then quickly passes, leaving no trace. The terms 'being' and 'non-being' cannot be applied to it.

If you survey the world with perfect intelligence and compassion, it seems like a vision which the human mind can never comprehend. The terms 'being' and 'non-being' cannot be applied to it.

With perfect intelligence and compassion which are beyond all limit, you have no attachments to things and persons. You have no ego; you do not regard yourself as a subject which knows, and things and persons as objects which are known. You are free from the hindrances of passion and intellect.

You do not yet vanish into nirvana, nor does nirvana abide in you, because nirvana transcends the duality of knowing and being known. But you are serene; you are free from all desire; you are cleansed of all corruption.

In this world, which is illusory, there is place for praise and blame. But in the ultimate reality, which is beyond the senses and beyond thought, what is there to praise?

Lankavatara Sutra I

Figments of the mind

The ignorant and foolish do not realize that the world is a
figment of the mind. Thus they cling to external objects; they
cling to notions of being and non-being, to notions of unity
and separateness, and to notions of eternity and time. They
think that they each have distinct selves. All this arises from
the mental habit of thinking logically, and thence discriminating between one thing and another. Thus their minds are
filled with illusions.

The conceptions in their minds are like mirages in the
desert, in which lakes of water appear before the eyes, but
are not real. These lakes are seen by animals, whose throats
are burning with thirst; the animals run towards them – not
knowing that they are hallucinations. In the same way the
ignorant and foolish, their minds burning with greed and
anger, chase external objects.

The conceptions in their minds are like dreams; and they
are like people asleep, who imagine that their dreams are real.
The conceptions in their minds are like pictures on a painter's
canvas. When people look at the canvas, they think they see
mountains and valleys; but in reality the canvas is flat.

Lankavatara Sutra I

Names, signs and ideas

Why do ignorant people cling to external objects, and wise people not cling to them?

In the first place ignorant people cling to names, signs and ideas. These names, signs and ideas push their minds into thinking that external objects are real. This sense of the reality of external objects appeals to the ego; they can see themselves as subjects, separate from the external objects.

The names, signs and ideas encourage them to designate some external objects as good, and some as bad; and they attach themselves to those they regard as good. This in turn fosters a sense of greed and possessiveness towards good objects; and greed engenders anger to anyone who threatens to harm or steal those objects.

In their folly they do not realize that all external objects are illusions – they are like the reflection of the moon on water. Similarly they do not realize that the ego is also illusory. So the names, signs and ideas have deluded their minds.

Lankavatara Sutra I

Words as tools of dualism

Most philosophers fail to recognize that the external world arises from the mind itself. And they do not realize that the ways in which the mind works, also arise from the mind itself. Thus philosophers erroneously imagine that conceptions within the mind correspond to external reality. For this reason philosophers cherish the dualism of this and that; they love to discriminate between one object and another.

The main tool for this dualism is language; words are used to discriminate between one object and another. And there are four types of words used for discrimination. First there are words indicating the distinguishing marks of external objects; these words operate like signs. Secondly there are words by which external objects and their surroundings are remembered; by this means external objects are assumed to have a continuous existence. Thirdly there are words which indicate the nature of a person's attachment to external objects. And finally there are abstract words which uphold the beliefs and prejudices on which dualism is based.

We may add a fifth type of word: these are words which, by common agreement, do not correspond to any external object. Examples include the hare's horns, the barren woman's child, and so on. This fifth type make plain that words are an artificial creation; in the land of perfect wisdom there are no words.

Lankavatara Sutra 2

The causes of apparent existence

They are two elements of causation which bring external objects into apparent existence: external elements and internal elements. The external elements include materials and tools, and also the workers who manipulate those tools and materials. So a jar is made from clay, a wheel, and a potter; a piece of cloth is made from yarn, a loom, and a weaver; butter is made from sour milk, a churn, and a man operating the churn – and so on. Since people are constantly working, new things appear one after the other in continuous succession. The internal elements include ignorance, desire and personality.

Causes may take six forms. There are indifference causes: this is where there are no internal elements, so things just come into apparent existence without human involvement. There are intention causes, where something comes into apparent existence just as particular humans intended. There are possibility causes, where internal and external elements combine in ways that humans cannot wholly predict. There are agency causes, where things are brought into apparent existence in obedience to some human authority, such as a king. There are subjectivity causes, where something is brought into existence solely within a mind. And there are manifesting causes, where a human brings something into apparent existence in order to manifest something else.

Lankavatara Sutra 2

Error and illusion

Error is itself an illusion. And since illusion cannot produce illusion, error cannot produce error. It is discrimination and attachment that produce evil thoughts. Moreover, illusion does not produce discrimination; on the contrary, discrimination produces illusion.

Error is not in itself a habit; discrimination and attachment are habits. Error is not in itself a fault; fault arises through the assertion of the ego, which causes discriminations to become confused.

Illusion is not in itself illusory; it has the reality of all external objects. External objects are not illusory because people are attached to them and cling to them; they are illusory because they are transient, appearing and disappearing with great speed. The illusory nature of external objects confuses the mind, causing one thought to contradict another.

Since people do not realize that the world is no more than a projection of the mind, they cling to external objects and to ideas of causation. In short, they cling to duality, in which they see themselves as subjects.

Lankavatara Sutra 2

Realism and nihilism

The thoughts of people in this world depend on one of two concepts: the concept of being, through which they take pleasure in realism; or the concept of non-being, through which they take pleasure in nihilism. In either case they imagine they are emancipated, whereas they are not.

Those who depend on the concept of being, regard the world as truly existing, and being caused by forces that are real. Those who depend on the concept of non-being, regard the world as not truly existing, and therefore not being caused by real forces.

This latter group admit the existence of greed, anger and folly; but they deny the existence of the things that produce greed, anger and folly. In this they are inconsistent: greed, anger and folly are no more real than the things that produce them.

The former group admit that things are transient. They see things as constantly appearing, and then passing away; they see things as constantly dividing, and then combining in different ways. But since they regard things as real, they are chained to this continuous state of flux, and therefore they are continuously disturbed by it.

Lankavatara Sutra 3

Seven kinds of emptiness

What is emptiness? There are seven kinds of emptiness.

There is emptiness of mutuality. When, for example, we say that a lecture hall is empty of elephants, we mean there is no mutual co-existence of the lecture hall and elephants. This is the lowest form of emptiness, and may be ignored.

There is emptiness of individuality. By this we mean that beings do not have individual characteristics. When there is emptiness of individuality, ideas of self, otherness, and bothness no longer hold good. Thus in truth all beings are empty of individuality.

There is emptiness of self-nature. By this we mean that all beings in themselves are not born. There is emptiness of inaction. By this we mean that all the elements that comprise a being are inactive. There is emptiness of action. By this we mean that the ego of any being is illusory; thus the action of any being has no deliberate purpose. There is emptiness of time. By this we mean that events in time are unpredictable because they have no purpose.

And there is the highest emptiness of ultimate reality. By this we mean that, when perfect wisdom is realized, the mind is empty of all conceptions and notions.

Lankavatara Sutra 3

Five levels of understanding

There are five levels of understanding: appearance, name, discrimination, right perception, and reality.

By appearance we mean that which appears to the senses,
as form, sound, odour, taste and touch. Out of these appearances we form notions of objects, to which we give names.
Thus we call a particular combination of appearances clay,
water, a jar, and so on. When we contrast one combination
of appearances with another, we are discriminating. Thus we
contrast an elephant with a horse, a man with a woman, and
so on.

Gradually we come to see these discriminations as mutu-
ally reinforcing, and therefore as empty of meaning. Then we
see them as they really are – as figments of the mind itself.
This is right perception.

When appearances and names are abandoned, when discrimination ceases, and when we recognize all things as figments of the mind, then we can encounter ultimate reality.
Reality has no image; it only has essence. Those who encounter ultimate reality, have attained perfect wisdom.

Lankavatara Sutra 4

Four kinds of knowledge

There are four kinds of knowledge: appearance knowledge, relative knowledge, perfect knowledge, and transcendental intelligence.

Appearance knowledge belongs to the ignorant and foolish, who are addicted to the notion of being and non-being, and who are frightened of letting this notion go. Appearance knowledge is loved by word-mongers, who revel in discriminating between things, and in making assertions about the nature of things.

Relative knowledge belongs to the thinking of philosophers. They like to consider the relationships between one object and another, and the relationship between an object and the subject observing it. In considering these relationships they use the mind's ability to find patterns and to make logical deductions.

Perfect knowledge belongs to enlightened people, who recognize that all things are figments of the mind; who understand the emptiness of all things; and who have passed through the five levels of understanding. Perfect knowledge belongs to enlightened people who are entirely free from the dualism of being and non-being, of birth and death, and of assertion and negation. They no longer see the world as subject to causation; they regard causation as a fable. To them the world is like a dream; it is the birth and death of a barren woman's child. To them nothing is evolving, and nothing is disappearing.

Lankavatara Sutra 4

The universal soul

The universal soul transcends all individual souls and their limitations. The universal soul is utterly pure; it is unchangeable; it is free from all faults; it is undisturbed by egoism; and it is unruffled by any kind of desire or aversion. The universal soul is like a great ocean. Its surface is moved by waves, but its depths are still. In itself the universal soul is devoid of personality and all the attributes of personality. But the motion on its surface makes it like an actor playing a variety of roles.

Between the universal soul and the individual soul lies the intuition. The intuition resides within the individual soul, but is guided and sustained by the universal soul. The intuition shares the universality of the universal soul, and shares its purity. It is through the intuition that goodness flows back and forth between the universal soul and the individual soul. The intuition is not transient; if it were, enlightenment would also be transient – and the wise would lose their wisdom. The intuition also shares the individuality of the individual soul.

Through the universal soul the intuition participates in transcendental intelligence. Transcendental intelligence is the inner state, in which perfect wisdom is realized. This realization takes place at the deepest level of consciousness.

Lankavatara Sutra 5, 6

Words and meanings

When reflecting upon transcendental intelligence, you should consider carefully the relationship of words and meanings.

Words express meanings. But they depend on discriminations and on memory, and also on the sounds of vowels and consonants through which meaning is conveyed from one person to another. Words are merely symbols, and can never fully express the intended meaning; indeed, the listener may misunderstand the speaker's intention altogether.

Meaning is illumined by words, as objects are illumined by a lamp. Words are like the lamp carried by a man to look at his property: he shines the lamp on his property, and declares that the property is his. Through words we can grasp the meaning of the Buddha's teachings, and thence be enlightened. Thus words are the means whereby perfect wisdom is grasped and attained.

But you should not become attached to the literal meaning of words; you should not cling to the notion that words and meanings correspond to one another. On the subject of nirvana, the word is an infinite distance from the meaning.

Lankavatara Sutra 6

Various kinds of teacher

When reflecting upon transcendental intelligence, you should also consider carefully the various kinds of teacher.

There are priests and preachers who perform rituals and ceremonies, and deliver eloquent sermons. These priests and preachers should not be treated with honour or regarded with reverence; they do not show you the way of contemplation, but they merely provide emotional excitement. Their clever manipulation of words, and their powerful rhetoric, in truth amount to no more than the babble of infants. They awaken sentiment, but stupefy the mind. They confuse their listeners with their dualistic views, in which the subject is differentiated from the object. Thus they can never save people from disease and sorrow, pain and despair.

There are philosophers who assume the reality of the world. They too should not be treated with honour or regarded with reverence. They may use hundreds of thousands of words, but they do not go beyond the concerns of the world and the human body. Thus their words imprison people within their present suffering.

And there are enlightened people. They teach that there is nothing beyond the mind itself; there is no difference between being and non-being; and there is no external world as the object of perception. They teach the solitude of reality.

Lankavatara Sutra 6

A gem radiating many colours

In order to become enlightened, you must grasp the teachings of those who are enlightened. You must understand how, in lonely places, and by means of their transcendental intelligence, they walked the path to nirvana. By understanding this, your mind will reflect and meditate upon it; and then the deepest level of your consciousness will transformed. And as the deepest level of your consciousness is transformed, you will perform the most wonderful deeds. You will become the master of your own mind. You will be like a gem radiating many colours. You will be able to enter the minds of other people, and thereby teach them what they need to know. Finally, by a process of gradual ascension, you will participate in the transcendental intelligence that enlightenment brings.

Nevertheless you should recognize that transcendental intelligence is not the same as perfect wisdom; it is the intuitive awareness of perfect wisdom. Perfect wisdom is the perfect state in which all images have ceased; it is the unity of the individual soul with the universal divine soul; it is serenity which cannot be disturbed.

Lankavatara Sutra 6

Four conditions for realization

In order to attain realization, and thereby possess perfect wisdom, you must fulfill four conditions.

First, you must recognize, and be fully convinced, that all beings in the world are merely figments of the mind; that all beings in the world are devoid of self; that all effort and motion are illusory.

Secondly, you must recognize, and be fully convinced, that all beings in the world are like forms seen in a dream, empty of substance and without origin.

Thirdly, you must recognize, and courageously accept, that your own mind and personality are themselves constructed by the mind, and therefore empty of substance and without origin. With this truth clearly in your mind, all images will cease, and you will enter the realm of truth.

Fourthly, you must have a true conception of perfect wisdom. It is not comparable to the perception of the senses, nor is it comparable to the concepts derived by discrimination and logic; both of these forms of knowledge presuppose a distinction between the subject which thinks, and the object which is the focus of thought – between the knower and the known. Realization is based on identity and unity. To attain realization you must be free from all attachments and all sense of self.

Lankavatara Sutra 7

Forms of attachment

There are three forms of attachment that are especially deep-seated in all human minds: greed, anger, and infatuation. These in turn are based on lust, fear and pride. Behind all these lie discrimination and desire, which are the twin roots of all attachments. Other forms of attachment include addiction to excitement, love of comfort, and hope for eternal life. If these attachments are completely broken, the mind will also be free from the yearning for detachment. In this way the net of detachment is swept away completely.

The ignorant and the foolish are like silkworms, who continue spinning their thread of discrimination, wrapping themselves and others within it; and they are utterly charmed by the prison they create. But the wise understand attachment and detachment, and they seek to break free from both; they understand the prison of discrimination, and they strive for the solitude of unity.

Realization occurs at the deepest level of consciousness. It is an inner experience, which has no connection with logical thought, or with words and ideas, or with philosophical speculation. It shines with its own clear light to reveal the error and folly of teachings constructed by the mind, and to render impotent the evil influences of those teachings. And it opens the way to the attainment of perfect wisdom.

Lankavatara Sutra 7

The context of meditation

In order to discard all discriminations and erroneous thoughts, you should go alone to some remote, secluded place, where you may meditate without interruption. There you should devote yourself entirely to advancing up the stages of meditation. It is only in solitude that you can do this. If the mind is constantly distracted, meditation becomes a matter of deliberate effort – and this is a hindrance. Only when the mind is alone and tranquil, is it able to abandon the discriminations of the external world, and seek realization within the inner realm. The lifelong habits of discriminative thinking cannot be broken easily or quickly.

Lankavatara Sutra 7

Four kinds of meditation

There are four kinds of meditation.

First, there is the meditation practised by the ignorant, who do not understand its purpose. They believe that meditation consists simply of sitting still with a vacant mind. This type of meditation is also practised by those who despise the body, regarding it merely as a vehicle of suffering and corruption, and yet cling to the ego; they believe that salvation from the body merely requires the cessation of thought.

Secondly, there is meditation devoted to the examination of meaning. This is practised by those who understand that the idea of the self, and hence the dualism of subject and object, is untenable. They meditate on the implications of forsaking the ego.

Thirdly, there is meditation on the ultimate essence of all things, and thence on the unity of the divine. By practising this type of meditation, you learn to forsake the ego; and in this process all forms and images disappear from the mind.

Fourthly, there is the meditation of those who are enlightened, in which perfect wisdom is contemplated. This meditation is not merely for the sake of the individual, but for the sake of all beings, because in this meditation all beings are made one.

Lankavatara Sutra 7

Concentrating the mind

To attain realization you must concentrate the mind, such that you identify your soul with perfect wisdom. In that effort of concentration you must annihilate all stray thoughts and concepts which relate to external objects; you must annihilate all ideas of individuality; you must annihilate all awareness of suffering; and you must annihilate all sense of impermanence. Instead you must cultivate the noblest ideas of egolessness, emptiness, and imagelessness; in this way all passion will drain away, and you will become utterly serene.

When this active effort of concentration is successful, it is followed by a more passive, receptive mental state, in which you enter the blissful land of perfect wisdom, and experience profound inner transformation. In this state you are filled with pure compassion for all living beings.

On this path to realization there is a great danger, of which you should beware. People sometimes think they can achieve serenity by suppressing the activities of the mind. This is an error, because even if all conscious thought is suppressed, the mental habits on which thought is based, still remain. Serenity is achieved not by suppressing thought, but by ridding thought of all discriminations and attachments.

Lankavatara Sutra 8

False conceptions of nirvana

Many people have false ideas about nirvana.

There are those who are currently suffering, or who fear suffering in the future – and regard nirvana as an escape from suffering, and as a recompense. They imagine that nirvana consists in the annihilation of the senses, and the pain which comes from the senses. They do not realize that the universal soul and nirvana are one and the same; nor do they realize that nirvana is not separate from this world of life and death. They talk of being saved; yet they cling to the notion of nirvana as outside the soul.

There are those who conceive of nirvana as the cessation of conscious thought, owing to an utter indifference to the external world. This indifference extinguishes all recollection of the past, and all awareness of the present – as if the lamp of the mind had been extinguished. This conception is misleading, because nirvana is not simply a matter of annihilation and vacuity.

There are those who conceive of nirvana as the mere stopping of discrimination. This, they contend, involves a great effort, in which the mind rids itself of all dualism: the dualism of subject and object, the knower and the known; the dualism of permanence and impermanence; and the dualism of good and evil. But nirvana can never be a matter of effort; if it were, the mind would be in a continuous state of disturbance and confusion.

Lankavatara Sutra 8

Nirvana as perfect wisdom and love

Many people think of nirvana as a state of eternal bliss; and
they go off to some remote place, with the intention of achieving this state. They recognize that the world is only a figment
of the mind, and that all discriminations come from the mind.
Thus they abandon all social relationships, and practise various
spiritual disciplines; and by these means they attain a degree
of bliss. Yet they are still clinging to the ego; so there is no
transformation at the deepest level of consciousness.

The Buddha's nirvana consists in recognizing that there is
nothing except the soul itself; in abandoning every kind of
discrimination; in suppressing all desire; and in breaking all
attachments to external objects. Nirvana is where all thought
is put away; where logic is no longer used; where even the
notion of truth is treated with indifference, because it causes
bewilderment; and where all propositions and theories are ignored. Nirvana is where all passions have subsided, and all
mental hindrances have been cleared away; where egolessness
is accepted; and where there is transformation at the deepest
level of consciousness, leading to realization.

Nirvana is where perfect wisdom is manifest, and perfect
love is expressed.

Lankavatara Sutra 8

The flash of insight

In the darkness of night, when a storm is raging and the clouds are thick, a flash of lightning brings a moment of brightness. In the same way a flash of spiritual insight can enlighten my soul.

At those moments I recognize that the power of goodness is weak, while the power of evil is strong. What can vanquish the power of evil, except a soul which has been enlightened by perfect wisdom?

I yearn to transcend the miseries of worldly existence. I yearn to lift the burden of sorrow from all living beings. I yearn to enjoy aeon upon aeon of bliss. Thus I constantly strive to enlighten my soul.

I have travelled across the world from city to city, trading precious objects. The soul enlightened by perfect wisdom is more precious than all the precious objects ever exchanged.

All other trees bear fruit, and then wither. But the tree of the enlightened soul constantly bears fruit, and never withers.

The enlightened soul is like a heroic warrior, giving protection from every danger. So why do people not seek the enlightenment of the soul?

Shantideva: Bodhicaryavatara 1.5, 6, 8, 11–13

Moving towards enlightenment

I distinguish between a soul that wishes to become enlightened, and a soul that is moving towards enlightenment. This
distinction is analogous to that between a person who wishes
to go to a certain place, and a person who is actually pro-
ceeding towards that place.

There is merit in wishing to become enlightened. But
there is far greater merit in moving towards enlightenment.
Now that I have resolved to move towards enlightenment,
even though I occasionally become weary or distracted,
streams of merit pour from the sky.

I wish to remove the suffering of every living being, en-
abling all to move towards enlightenment. I wish to align my
soul with the universal soul, which is the source of pure
happiness in the world. My concern for the welfare of others
gains me greater merit than any act of worship.

I wish to share my joy with those starved of joy; I wish
to share my salvation with those who are oppressed; by the
shattering of illusion in my mind, I wish to shatter illusion
in the minds of others.

Shantideva: Bodhicaryavatara 1.15–16, 19, 22, 25–27, 29–30

Confession of sin

I frequently sin. I possess no spiritual wealth. I have nothing
to offer in worship. I depend wholly on the divine powers. I
entrust myself wholly to them.

Take possession of me, divine powers; I am your slave.
When you make me your own, I become fearless. I act for
the benefit of others. I repent of my past sins, and I commit
myself never to sin again.

For countless aeons, from one birth to the next, I have
committed terrible sins, causing great injury to other living
beings. I have rejoiced in my own evil. Now I realize what I
have done, and I am tormented by remorse.

In my arrogance I have harmed my mother and father in
every life – so I have harmed countless mothers and fathers.
In every life I have harmed many people who deserved respect
– so I have harmed countless people worthy of respect. In
body, speech and mind I have injured people. I confess it all.

How can I escape the consequences of my sins? Divine
powers, I am frightened. Do not let me die until my past evil
has been wiped out. Rescue me quickly.

Shantideva: Bodhicaryavatara 2.7–9, 28–33

Anticipating death

Death pays no heed to what has been done or not done. Death strikes not only the sick, but also those who are well. Death comes like a thunderbolt from nowhere.

I have done evil to my friends, as well as to my enemies. I did not understand what I was doing. But when death comes, all opportunity to make amends will have gone. Those whom I loathe, will die; those whom I love, will die; I shall die; all will die.

Every experience, as soon as it is complete, becomes a memory; it is like an image in a dream; it can never be seen again. Many people whom I have known, friends and enemies, have died; so they are now only memories. Yet the consequences of their evil conduct still remain. I too will die, and become only a memory; but the consequences of my evil will remain. If only I had recognized this! In a state of delusion, desire or aversion, I have committed countless sins.

Night and day, without respite, life passes; every moment more of life is lost. Life never grows longer; it is always shortening. And as death approaches, even though I shall be surrounded by my family, I must endure its agonies alone. When the messenger of death arrives, what good is a relative, what good is a friend? Merit alone is the only defence – and I have not acquired enough.

Shantideva: Bodhicaryavatara 2.34–42

A herb that always heals

May I be medicine for the sick; let me be both their doctor and their nurse, healing every disease so that it never recurs. May I be food for the hungry and drink for the thirsty; in times of famine let me provide for every person's needs. May I be treasure for the poor; let me provide wealth from an inexhaustible source.

Without regret I give up any comfort for the sake of others. I know that I must abandon comforts in order to attain enlightenment; and enlightenment is my deepest wish. If I must give up all material possessions, I wish to hand them to other living beings.

I hand over my body itself to others. Let them beat it, mock it, and splatter it with dirt, if they wish. Let them use my body for whatever purpose they choose. My body means nothing to me.

Some people make false accusations against me; others strive to impoverish me; and others try to destroy my reputation. My wish for them is that they share in my enlightenment.

May I protect the unprotected. May I be the boat that carries people across troubled waters. May I be a light for those in darkness. May I be a bed for those in need of rest. May I be a servant for those who need service. May I be a jewel that grants wishes, a spell that always works, a herb that always heals, and a cow that is always in milk.

Shantideva: Bodhicaryavatara 3.7–13, 16–19

A wild elephant

I must guard my mind with great care, so that it does not wander. A wild elephant wandering through the jungle does not cause as much devastation as a wandering mind. If the wild elephant can be tethered, the devastation ceases; similarly I must tether my mind.

Every fear and every form of suffering arises from within the mind. It is the mind that fashions the torments of hell. It is the mind that invents the scalding irons, and every other instrument of torture. Every evil thing stems from mental evil; nothing is dangerous except the mind.

Perfect generosity would make the world free from poverty. Thus poverty exists because human minds are mean. Perfect generosity would occur if people ceased to regard anything as their own. So poverty occurs because people regard themselves as owners.

Perfect morality would make the world free from killing. If people were moral, animals and fish would be safe from human weapons. Killing occurs because human minds are immoral. If immorality were slain, slaying would cease.

I cannot control external events; but I can control my mind. If my mind is controlled, I shall be free from suffering – and so shall have no cause for fear.

Shantideva: Bodhicaryavatara 5.1–3, 7–12, 14

An open wound

If I had an open wound, and found myself in a crowd, I should guard the wound with great care. In the same way I shall guard my mind with great care from evil influences. Let my wealth decay, let my reputation be destroyed, let my body die; but let my mind always be protected.

When a man is weak with illness, he is not fit for work. In the same way, when a mind is weakened by distraction, it cannot strive for enlightenment. A cracked jar cannot hold water; in the same way a distracted mind cannot hear, meditate upon, and memorize the truth. Many intelligent men and women, though they have possessed faith, and though they have strived hard, have failed to attain enlightenment because they did not guard their minds.

I shall constantly watch over my mind. If it starts to wander, I shall pull it back. Not even for a moment will I allow my concentration to lapse. In every task which I undertake, I shall concentrate only on that task until it is completed. In this way I shall do everything well.

When I am in conversation, I shall guard against any enthusiasm for worthless gossip, and I shall watch for any tendency towards idle curiosity. When I am sitting on the ground, I shall quell any urge to engage in pointless activities, such as pulling at the grass or drawing lines on the earth. When I feel moved to speak, I shall first examine what I want to say; and only when I am confident that my words will be kind and wise, shall I open my mouth.

Shantideva: Bodhicaryavatara 5.19, 22, 24–26, 41–47

A block of wood

When I observe that my mind is either attracted or repelled, I shall neither speak nor act, but remain like a block of wood.

When I am tempted to promote myself at the expense of others, I shall remain like a block of wood. Equally when I am tempted to disparage others, speaking about them with disdain and contempt, I shall remain like a block of wood.

When I am tempted to pursue wealth, honour or fame, and when I crave the attention of others, I shall remain like a block of wood.

When my mouth yearns to speak at length, out of pride in the sagacity of my own views, rather than for the good of others, I shall remain like a block of wood.

When I notice that my thoughts are becoming impure, or I am engaged in some pointless activity, I shall remain like a block of wood.

I shall be determined and confident, reliable and diligent in doing good. I shall be humble and meek towards others, treating all with respect. I shall be both calm and eager in offering people help.

I shall not be deterred or confused by the conflicting demands of the foolish, but I shall pity them for their folly. I shall make my own decisions, according to my own convictions, with a mind free from illusion.

Shantideva: Bodhicaryavatara 5.48, 50–52, 54–57

A friend to the world

When I have mastered my own nature, I shall always have a smiling face. I shall never frown or scowl, but I shall be a friend to the whole world.

I shall never hurl furniture in anger or frustration; nor shall I knock loudly on doors to call people. I shall prefer silence to noise. Just as a crane, or a cat, or a thief, moves quietly and gently, so shall I.

I shall listen with respect to the advice of the wise, even when I have not sought it. I shall regard myself as the pupil of everyone who has greater wisdom than I have.

I shall be quick to express gratitude to those who help me. I shall offer encouragement to every good intention. And I shall be generous in praising every achievement.

I shall speak of the virtues of others in their absence, and repeat my words in their presence, taking pleasure in their gratification. When others praise me, I shall reflect on whether their praise is deserved.

I shall measure my words with care, ensuring that they are clear in meaning, pleasant to hear, and rooted in compassion. When I speak, I shall look into the eyes of my listener, expressing love with my own eyes.

Shantideva: Bodhicaryavatara 5.71–76, 79–80

Poison in the mind

There is no evil equal to hatred, and no virtue equal to compassion. Therefore I shall nurture compassion by every means.

If the dart of hatred has pierced the heart, the mind can find no peace, it can enjoy no pleasure, it cannot rest, and it cannot feel safe and secure.

When people are disfigured with hatred, their friends shrink from them, and their own relatives yearn for their death. They may do good to others, but they are not honoured for it. In short, hatred destroys those who hate.

Those who understand the harm that hatred does, and who persistently strive to suppress it, are happy in this life and the next. Hatred is the most deadly enemy, and must be destroyed.

When hatred has entered me, I have felt as if I had eaten poison. Within my mind it destroyed that which was good, and caused evil to thrive. It seemed to be murdering me. Therefore I have resolved to poison this poison, murder this murderer.

Shantideva: Bodhicaryavatara 6.2–8

Bearing hardship

No hardship is truly hard to bear, if it is borne frequently and with patience. Minor discomforts cease to be uncomfortable; and even major discomforts become tolerable.

I shall learn to ignore the irritation of bugs, gnats and mosquitoes. Hunger and thirst will not disturb me. Even a persistent itch will not annoy me. All these things I shall regard as trivial.

Cold and heat, rain and wind, travel and disease, imprisonment and beatings – I shall be indifferent to them all. If I allow myself to be distressed by them, then my distress will grow until it overwhelms me.

Patience in the face of hardship is courage; distress at hardship is cowardice. So in the face of hardship I shall be a warrior who can never be vanquished.

I shall acquire such serenity of mind that no pain can disturb me. I shall wear spiritual armour, so even the hardest blows will not shake me. Yes, I shall be a hero.

More than that, I shall actually welcome suffering, because suffering breeds compassion for all who suffer. Even towards those who cause me suffering, I shall feel no anger; instead, I shall try to understand the suffering within them, which prompts them to cause suffering to others.

Shantideva: Bodhicaryavatara 6.14–16, 18–22

The causes and consequences of anger

People do not become angry because they have decided to
become angry; anger does not well up within the breast, because the mind has commanded it to well up. People respond
angrily in particular situations because they have been subject
to evil influences in the past, and themselves have committed
evil in the past. Anger is a consequence of evil, and does not
exist independently from evil.

It is sometimes said that suppressing anger is pointless, because people cannot suppress that which is within them. But
since anger is the consequence of evil, it can be suppressed
by attacking evil. When evil is overcome, anger will cease.

When I see a friend or an enemy behaving angrily, I shall
not be upset. I shall remind myself that this person has not
chosen to be angry. I shall reflect on the evil that underlies
the anger. And I shall assure myself that no one wants to be
evil, and therefore no one wants to be angry.

Anger causes people to torment themselves. They pick up
thorns, and prick their skin. They refuse food. Some even
commit suicide, hanging themselves, throwing themselves
off cliffs, or taking some deadly poison. When I see the suffering which anger causes to angry people, I feel nothing
but pity.

Shantideva: Bodhicaryavatara 6.24–25, 32–36, 38

Praise and insult

Praise, reputation and honour lead neither to merit nor to longevity; they confer neither strength nor protection against disease; and they do not give bodily pleasure. They only give pleasure to the mind – and this could more easily be obtained by drunkenness, gambling and other vices.

For the benefit of acquiring praise, reputation and honour, people forgo many other benefits. They even risk their lives. Yet can words of praise be eaten? Can reputation and honour give pleasure to the dying?

Children howl with distress when their toys are broken; so adults howl when their reputation is sullied. Yet I refuse to be affected by praise or insult. If other people take delight in me, I take pleasure only in their delight.

If I were to take the praise of others to heart, I should become complacent. The sense of urgency to improve myself would be dulled. I should become jealous at those who won greater praise, and resentful at those who enjoyed greater success.

So equally those who insult and mock me, confer on me great benefit. They save me from descending into misery.

Shantideva: Bodhicaryavatara 6.90–94, 98–99

Attachment to people and status

I shall seek to stabilize my mind through concentrated meditation; I shall not allow myself to be distracted. Distraction
does not occur if the body and the mind are under control.
Thus I shall renounce all worldly attachments, and ignore all
wandering thoughts.

The hardest attachment to renounce is attachment to
people. I must constantly remind myself that all people are
transient; and when loved ones die, I shall not see them again
for many thousands of lives. Grief at the death of a loved one
destroys all concentration; the mind is consumed with longing to see that person again, and yet that longing cannot be
satisfied. And during the period of grief, the remainder of life
is getting shorter — so the loss of the loved one may cause
the loss of the Way.

The next hardest attachment to renounce is attachment to
status. Yet attachment to status induces jealousy towards those
who are superior, rivalry towards those who are equal, and
arrogance towards those who are inferior. It also induces in-
toxication when praise is given, and hatred when adverse crit-
icisms are made.

Shantideva: Bodhicaryavatara 8. 1–2, 5–6, 8, 12

Freedom from conflict and passion

Human beings are born alone, and die alone; the agonies of birth and death cannot be shared. At the moment of birth and the moment of death, what help are relatives and friends? Life is a lodging between birth and death.

I have freed myself from friends and relatives; I have freed myself from all sources of conflict. I am utterly alone in this body. I have died to the world, and no one grieved at my death. Nothing can now distress me; nothing can now distract me.

I shall always live alone. Solitude delights me, and frees me from anxiety. Solitude calms me. In solitude I can focus my mind on a single point; I can tame my mind, so that it can meditate without wandering.

I suppress all passion. Passions bring misfortune in this life and the next. No sword, no poison, no fire, no precipice, no hateful enemy can cause the torment which passion causes. The delight which I take in solitude, far exceeds any sensual enjoyment which passion can bring – and, besides, this enjoyment is always accompanied by contention and strife. How much better to be alone in a tranquil forest, or on a quiet mountain!

Shantideva: Bodhicaryavatara 8.33–34, 36–40, 84–86

Solitude and love

In solitude I spend my time as I please. And in solitude I live where I please: in a deserted hut, beneath a tree, or in a cave. I do not exhaust myself providing for a family and protecting a house and land; I am free from care. I behave as I choose. Bound to no one, I enjoy happiness and contentment which would evoke envy even in a king. In solitude my mind is calm, so I can meditate in peace; and through meditation I move towards enlightenment.

I meditate on the equality of myself and others, saying to myself: 'All experience suffering and happiness in equal measure. I care for others as much as I care for myself.' Just as the body, with its many organs and its limbs, is a single entity, so all living beings form a single entity. And just as the health or sickness of one part of the body affects the whole, so the happiness or suffering of one living being affects all living beings.

It is true that the suffering of other living beings does not actually distress me. Yet I regard the suffering of any living being as intolerable, because of the regard I have for myself; I love myself, so I love all beings. Thus I wish to dispel suffering from others, as much as I wish to dispel it from myself; I want others to be happy, because I myself want to be happy.

Shantideva: Bodhicaryavatara 8.87–95

Conventional and ultimate truth

In order to put an end to suffering I should deepen my understanding of truth.

It is agreed that there are two truths: the conventional and the ultimate. The truth grasped by the intellect is conventional; the reality lying beyond the intellect is ultimate. In the light of this distinction, it is possible to distinguish two types of people: those who are undeveloped spiritually; and those who are developed spiritually. The conventional truth, apprehended by those who are spiritually undeveloped, is superseded by the ultimate truth, apprehended by the spiritually developed.

Ordinary people, who are undeveloped, look at external objects, and imagine them to be real. Those who are developed, know that all external objects are illusions. Objective knowledge of external objects is not genuine knowledge; it is objective only in the sense that many people agree on it. But this consensus is wrong. In the same way, ordinary people agree that impure thoughts are pure; and they are wrong on that also.

Shantideva: Bodhicaryavatara 9. 1—6

Understanding illusion

People ask: 'If a living being is an illusion, how is it reborn after it has died?' I answer: 'Even an illusion persists for as long as the causes for it persist.'

People ask: 'If consciousness is an illusion, then surely murdering a human being is not a crime?' I answer: 'On the contrary, good and evil arise when one is endowed with the illusion of consciousness.'

People ask: 'What produces the illusion of consciousness?' I answer: 'Every cause that has an effect, produces the illusion of consciousness.'

People ask: 'If perception is illusory, how is an illusion perceived?' I answer: 'Illusion is perceived by that which is not illusory.'

People ask: 'What is the point of understanding that illusions are illusory?' I answer: 'Through understanding that illusions are illusory, enlightenment is attained.'

Shantideva: Bodhicaryavatara 9.9–13, 15–16, 40

No self

Fear arises because I believe that the self exists. Since the self is illusory, fear is irrational; and when I truly understand this, I shall never be frightened.

The teeth, hair and nails are not the self; nor are the bones, the blood, the mucus and the phlegm. The marrow and the sweat are not the self; nor are the excrement and the urine. The flesh and the sinews are not the self; nor are the heat and the wind. The orifices are not the self, nor are any forms of consciousness.

If consciousness of sound were the self, then sound would be perceived at all times. But when there is silence, there is no consciousness of sound; so it cannot be the self.

If not being conscious of anything were the self, then the self would be no more than a block of wood. If, on the other hand, being conscious of something were the self, then the self would disappear when I fell asleep.

The present mind is not the self, because the present mind only exists for a moment. The future mind is not the self, because it does not yet exist.

Thus there is no body, and there is no self.

Shantideva: Bodhicaryavatara 9.56–61, 68, 73, 82

Happiness for all

May the path towards enlightenment be filled with people.

Through my love and compassion, may all those who are currently suffering in body and mind, plunge into an ocean of happiness and joy. And as long as the cycle of birth and rebirth remains, may their happiness never fade.

May those who are cold, find warmth. May those who are sick with fever, be cooled by rain-clouds of comfort.

May animals cease to eat one another, so that every animal may be free from fear. May the hungry be fed, and the filthy bathed in streams of milk. May the blind see, the deaf hear, and pregnant mothers give birth without pain. May the naked be clothed, the thirsty receive drink, and the ugly be made beautiful. May all living beings have everything that their hearts desire.

May the frightened be saved from fear, the oppressed be saved from tyranny, and the anxious feel secure. May the sick be made well, the weak be made strong, and the hateful be made loving.

May every town and village offer hospitality to the traveller. May every plan succeed.

Shantideva: Bodhicaryavatara 10. 1–3, 17–23

Monks, nuns and scholars

May monks enjoy solitude, and find joy in obeying their teachers; may their minds be supple and concentrated, so they may meditate deeply.

May nuns receive material support, and may they never bicker or be harassed; may they always observe the highest standards of morality. May they live together in perfect unity.

May those whose conduct is wrong, be jolted into seeing the need to change. May they take pleasure in changing their ways, so they put every kind of evil behind them. May they then attain a good rebirth, and in future lives may their good behaviour be sustained.

May scholars be given food, so they can devote themselves to study. May their mental states always be pure; and may the fruits of their scholarship be widely known.

May the whole universe attain enlightenment, and every soul be absorbed into the universal soul. In the meantime, as long as the world persists, and as long as I remain, may I strive to destroy all suffering.

Shantideva: Bodhicaryavatara 10.43–47, 55

The intuition leading to enlightenment

The intuition which leads to enlightenment, is as wide as the oceans; it is as fluid and as accommodating as water itself. This intuition is utterly profound, and inconceivably mysterious.

When this intuition is fixed on objects, it ceases to be fluid and accommodating; it loses its true nature. It begins to perceive differences between objects; it sees objects within space; and it becomes aware of the entire universe. It then develops conceptions – patterns of thought – which accord with these eternal perceptions. And finally it perceives itself as a sentient being – and thus develops an ego.

To the enlightened soul space is like foam tossed about on the waves of a great sea. Thus the unenlightened soul is under the illusion that this foam is permanent, not transient.

Surangama Sutra

One Way and different circumstances

All living beings wish to return to their origins in which
there is perfect unity. People may say there are many different
ways of achieving this; and this may appear to be the case.
But in truth there is only one Way; this is the Way taught by
all enlightened teachers. It is a way that leads to total serenity.

There are, however, differences in the circumstances in
which people try to follow the Way. Some circumstances make
it easy to follow the Way, while others make it difficult.

Surangama Sutra

Sight, words, fragrances and tastes

The sense of sight, and the conceptions that appear in people's minds as a consequence of the sense of sight, become entangled with the objects of sight. This process prevents the mind from thinking clearly; thus the sense of sight hinders the attainment of perfect wisdom.

The sounds of words are inclined to fascinate people; they appreciate a refined style of writing and speaking; they like to formulate precise definitions, distinguishing the meaning of one word from another. All this inhibits people from perceiving the underlying unity of all phenomena; thus the sense of hearing hinders the attainment of perfect wisdom.

People say that a certain object is fragrant when they associate the sensation of fragrance with the perception of that object. When sensation and perception are linked, people's minds become entangled with fragrant objects. This process prevents the mind from thinking clearly; thus the sense of smell hinders the attainment of perfect wisdom.

Tastes do not last; they exist only as long as the tasty object is present. People are inclined to think of taste only in terms of tasty objects, not realizing that the capacity to taste is permanent. This failure to distinguish between taste and the sense of taste confuses the mind; thus the sense of taste hinders the attainment of perfect wisdom.

Surangama Sutra

Emotions and conceptions

Emotions arise through contact with other living beings; where there is no contact, there is no emotion. People find it difficult to avoid contact with other beings, and so they are constantly disturbed by emotions. Thus the existence of emotions hinders the attainment of perfect wisdom.

As soon as people admit the conception of other beings into their minds, they find themselves assuming that the beings exist. If they are not aware of the process of causation, they also assume that these beings exist in themselves, as separate and independent entities. This hinders the attainment of perfect wisdom.

All people have seen their essential nature, but few have understood it. Most people only perceive the surface; their minds cannot penetrate below the surface. This failure to understand their essential nature hinders the attainment of perfect wisdom.

Surangama Sutra

Breath, thoughts, eyes and ears

Breathing is a spontaneous, involuntary activity; but it is affected by moods and emotions. Until the breath is perfectly co-ordinated with the mind, people cannot attain a state of tranquillity. Co-ordinating the breath with the mind is not merely a matter of concentrating on inhaling and exhaling. Thus the activity of breathing hinders the attainment of perfect wisdom.

The intelligent mind is filled with thoughts. Inevitably there is some conflict between thoughts; and these conflicts constantly disturb the mind. The conflicts are so numerous and deep that they cannot all be resolved. Thus the activity of thinking hinders the attainment of perfect wisdom.

Awareness of sights within the mind depends on the eye. The eye is no more than a physical organ; and for this reason we cannot be sure that the sights in the mind correspond to the objects being seen. This lack of confidence disturbs the mind. Thus the organ of the eye hinders the attainment of perfect wisdom.

If the ear could hear all that could be heard, it would hear all that is happening in other universes, and it would also hear the divine powers in action. But most ears hear only nearby sounds, and so give a very partial impression of all that is happening. Thus the organ of the ear hinders the attainment of perfect wisdom.

Surangama Sutra

Meditating on the elements

If people meditate on the element of earth, their minds will be thinking of hardness and softness – the hardness of rock, and the softness of soil. These are concepts that are concerned with change and impermanence; so by meditating on earth, people think of themselves as subject to change and impermanence. For this reason meditating on earth does not bring perfect wisdom.

If people meditate on the element of water, their minds will be thinking of fluidity and flow. These are concepts that are concerned with change and impermanence; so by meditating on water, people think of themselves as subject to change and impermanence. For this reason meditating on water does not bring perfect wisdom.

If people meditate on the element of fire, their minds will be thinking of destruction and pain. These are concepts that are concerned with change and impermanence; so by meditating on fire, people think of themselves as subject to change and impermanence. For this reason meditating on fire does not bring perfect wisdom.

If people meditate on the element of wind, their minds will be thinking of motion and stillness. These are concepts that are concerned with change and impermanence; so by meditating on wind, people think of themselves as subject to change and impermanence. For this reason meditating on wind does not bring perfect wisdom.

Surangama Sutra

Meditating on space and consciousness

If people meditate on pure space, their thoughts become thin and hazy. And such thoughts cannot bring perfect wisdom.

If people meditate on pure consciousness, their thoughts become focused on the impermanence of all thought; and their thoughts about thought will themselves be impermanent, passing away almost as soon as they have appeared. Thus their consciousness will become quite unreal and fantastic. Such thoughts cannot bring perfect wisdom.

If people meditate upon the teaching that all things are impermanent, these meditations hold them within the cycle of death and rebirth. Such meditations are not in conformity with the permanence of perfect wisdom.

Surangama Sutra

Seeds of transcendence

There are sermons delivered without the sounds of words. These sermons are enlightening to those who have learnt to control their minds in previous lives; but they are useless to novices who are dependent on concepts and definitions and eloquence to maintain their interest. So sermons without words cannot help the majority of people in the attainment of perfect wisdom.

Obeying the precepts of morality is a vital part of following the Way. Yet morality alone is not sufficient for the attainment of perfect wisdom.

The seeds of spiritual transcendence are planted over many lives. A novice may plant the seeds of transcendence in this life; but they will not bear fruit in this life. The reason is that the habit of thinking logically, in which the mind is constantly discriminating between one object and another, is so strong that it cannot be broken in a single lifetime; and logical thought perturbs the mind, hindering the attainment of perfect wisdom.

The logical, discriminating mind may enjoy periods of serenity, when the circumstances are tranquil. But this serenity is transient; and as circumstances change, disturbance returns.

Surangama Sutra

Transcending noise and silence

The essence of sound is felt in both noise and silence; when noise subsides into silence, the essence of sound passes from existence to non-existence. When there is no sound, people are apt to conclude there is no hearing; but even in silence the ears and the mind are prepared to hear. Indeed, when there is no sound, the hearing is most alert; and when there is sound, the hearing is most relaxed. Only by transcending both noise and silence can people attain stability and permanence.

In dreams, when the mind has become quiet, the hearing is still alert. This shows that hearing can go beyond the conscious sphere of body, speech and mind. In truth, the faculty of hearing is capable of receiving spiritual sound; and when people hear spiritual sound, they have transcended noise and silence. But most people are deaf to spiritual sound, so they only hear noise and silence – which constantly disturb the mind.

Surangama Sutra

External and internal perceptions

There was a disciple who had a wonderful memory. Yet he was unable to avoid falling into evil; he was adrift on a merciless sea. The reason was that he learnt all the teachings of Gautama Buddha, even the most secret teachings, without attempting to save himself from desires and attachments. His mind became a tower of religious knowledge, in which he was imprisoned. This disciple needed to turn his mind away from the words of Gautama Buddha, and towards himself. He needed to listen to the Way within his own mind, and then put into practice what he heard.

Spiritual hearing cannot be acquired until the mind and the will are under control. When you try to hear spiritually, and when you start to reflect on what you hear, there is always a danger that an external sound will interrupt you, and disturb your mind. Thus spiritual hearing depends on controlling the mind to such a degree that external sounds are excluded, and only spiritual sounds are heard.

When you have learnt to hear spiritually, and then return to hearing external sounds, you realize that external sounds are illusory, and only spiritual sounds are true. And this in turn leads you to conclude that all external perceptions – through seeing, smelling, tasting and touching, as well as hearing – are illusory; and only internal perceptions are true.

Surangama Sutra

The body's choice

I know that this body is made of flesh and blood, mixed with consciousness. It is a vessel for those who want freedom; and it is also a vessel for those who want sin.

I know that this body can choose between profit and loss, good and evil, eternal bliss or eternal misery. I want freedom from all bondage; I realize that this is difficult to attain, but I know that freedom leads to bliss.

I know that the means of attaining freedom is the teacher. I must have a spiritual bond with my teacher, in which I obey his instructions without compromise.

I know that to attain freedom my mind must meditate with great intensity on impermanence and death, on the consequences of different actions, and on the pain of constant flux. The mind must develop a yearning for freedom, and a commitment to observe the highest moral precepts.

I know that I must keep watch over my eyes. When my eyes stray, I must put them right at once. I know that I must dedicate myself to the good of all, so that all my actions are motivated by love and compassion.

Milarepa 2.4

The state of serenity

I must seek to discover how to lose the self. I shall seek to understand the self by means of rational inquiry and the study of great teachings, and also by means of metaphors and images. And when I understand the self, I shall also understand that the self does not exist.

When I understand that the self does not exist, my mind will enter a state of serenity. When my mind is serene, discriminating thought will cease and conceptual distinctions will disappear. I shall then become oblivious to the passing of time – and will have to be reminded of it by others.

I shall maintain this state of serenity by means of vigilance and awareness; I shall not allow my mind to be distracted, or to sink in passivity. By the strength of my vigilance and awareness I shall keep my mind pure and clear – for purity and clarity are the essential elements of serenity.

Through the purity and clarity of my mind I shall gain perfect wisdom. I shall have visions, in which I shall see the various forms of divinity. And then I shall perceive that these forms are without substance, and are merely figments of the mind.

Milarepa 2.4

A summary of spiritual knowledge

Let me summarize my spiritual knowledge.

First, a state of mental serenity, combined with a discerning intellect, are required for attaining perfect wisdom.

Secondly, all meditation must be rooted in compassion and love; and compassion and love must bear fruit in action.

Thirdly, all discriminating thought must cease, and all conceptual distinctions must disappear.

Fourthly, the self must be recognized as illusory; so the distinction between the self and other is also recognized as illusory.

Those who are starving, cannot be fed by knowledge of food, but must eat. Similarly, those who seek perfect wisdom, will not be satisfied merely by knowing how to attain it; they must actually attain it. Perfect wisdom cannot be attained unless the mind is pure, and every deed is good. There can be no respite from this.

So I shall subdue my body, greatly reducing the amount of food I eat; and I shall subdue my mind, eliminating all anxiety and excitement.

Milarepa 2.4

The sun rising on snowy mountains

Great teacher, who is fully enlightened, you listen to my stumbling words, in which I express my spiritual knowledge and insights. I beg you to be patient with my faults, my ignorance, and my errors. Please correct them according to the Way.

Your compassion is like the sun. Its rays burn up my faults, my ignorance, and my errors. Its warmth and light open the lotus of my soul. And as the lotus opens, so I release the fragrance of my gratitude. No fragrance is sweeter

than my gratitude for your teaching. To you I render perpetual homage.

Under your guidance I shall strive towards the limit of perfection. May my meditation bear fruit for all living beings.

You, great teacher, are good news. I bow before you. Yes, you are like the sun rising on the dark, snowy mountains.

Milarepa 2.4

A disciple's request and a teacher's reply

I say this to my teacher: 'Compassionate master, allow me to return to my home. I wish to see if anything is left of my possessions, and to see if my house is in ruins or still standing. I wish to see if rain falls through the roof of the temple, onto the sacred texts; and to see if the fertile fields are now overrun by weeds. I wish to see if my mother's mortal body is still strong and free from disease; to see if my sister is now a wandering beggar; to see if my uncle, a great soldier, is still alive; to see if my ferocious aunt is now dead; to see if the old priest still functions. Above all, I yearn for my mother, who brought me, my body and my mind, into the world; my longing for her is unbearable.'

My teacher replies: 'When you first came to me, you declared that you were no longer attached to your homeland, or to anyone who lived there. Now you say that you wish to return. I shall let you go. When you come back to me, remember this: if you find me asleep, it is a sign that we should not speak to each other again in this life. Yet the sun rising at this moment is a sign that you will be a light to others; the rays of the sun now striking my head tell me that you will convey the true teachings far and wide. The arrival of my maidservant with food tells me that you will constantly receive spiritual nourishment. All that is required, is for me to release you.'

Milarepa 2.5

Teaching and knowing

My teacher continues: 'The instructions which I have transmitted to you, were transmitted to me by my teacher. You in
turn must transmit them to your disciples. This line of trans-
mission must be maintained for thirteen generations. Do not
transmit these instructions in return for food or wealth, or to
please the listeners; this will incur the wrath of the angels.
Keep these instructions in your heart, and practise them. If
people come to you who are meant to come to you, welcome
them as disciples, even if they have no gifts to offer. Teach
all your disciples with sensitivity to their spiritual condition.

'If you look at the lives of the enlightened teachers, you
see that the desire for more instruction is a distraction. So
keep what I have already taught you, safely in your heart. Too
many lessons, without time to enact what is taught, are like
many trees without fruit. Every lesson may convey knowledge; but no lesson can convey ultimate truth. To know
every teaching that has ever been given, is not to know the
truth. Too much explanation brings no spiritual benefit; practising what is taught, is the source of spiritual wealth. If you
wish to be rich, enact what you know. The Way purifies the
mind; if you wish to be pure, follow it.

'A mind that is free from all attachment, is a mind that is
serene; a mind that is full of worldly concerns, is a mind that
is miserable. Your body is the sanctuary of the mind; meditation without distraction brings health to both.'

                                                    Milarepa 2.5

The nectar of bliss and the tree of insight

I go to my homeland as a beggar a seeker. The twelve angels of the mountain will come to meet me; the angels of the sky and the earth and the realm beneath the earth will escort me. Enlightenment is my companion, so I have nothing to fear from thieves and robbers.

I invoke my teacher, my compassionate master, offering this prayer: 'Guide me not only in this life, but in the next life also. Protect me from all danger, physical, moral and spiritual. Empower me with compassion and with knowledge. Grant me a long life, free from illness. Give me the strength to live in solitude in the mountains.'

I hear my teacher's reply: 'The silent voice of truth within your heart is the nectar of bliss. The knowledge growing in your mind is the tree of insight, rooted in wisdom and covered with the leaves of spiritual transformation. My words will live in your heart, and never be forgotten. The blessings of the angels will penetrate to the very foundations of your life.'

Milarepa 2.5

Village, cave and mountain

My teacher continued: 'Tomorrow the angels will urge you forward to your homeland. In your house and field you have a teacher of transient illusion. In your aunt, your sister and your relatives you have a master who dissolves illusion. In the cave in the nearby mountain, where you will live, you have a market where you can barter thought for nirvana. In your heart and your mind, you have a monastery where all enlightened teachers unite.

'In your village the people will not love you; so you will be able to practise love without reward. In the dark seclusion of your cave, without humans or even dogs for company, you will light the torch that illuminates the truth. On the mountain, where you will gather food without begging, you will be blessed with a peaceful heart.

'Ultimately you will go to a crystal palace, where you will witness your own spiritual victory. Through following the Way with all your heart, you will become a spiritual king. By carrying out all my instructions, you will have the treasure of enlightenment. Through the sacred teachings which form the heart of every angel, you will find the frontier between flux and nirvana.

'May future disciples in every generation be equally blessed; may those blessings be constant and unchanging.'

Milarepa 2.5

Mother and son

My mother says: 'I welcome you, my son; you possess great courage and powers of endurance, and you are gentle and loyal in your affection. Blessed son, drink the nectar of your teacher, the wine of perfect wisdom, that you may be wholly satisfied – and then depart. May we meet again as friends in the pure land of the Buddha.

'Do not forget us, your father and mother. We sought to feed your heart with true teachings; you ate your fill, and digested them. May we meet again as friends in the pure land of the Buddha.

'Do not forget our compassion. Let our kindness and compassion be your model. Wear as your cloak the breath of angels, and let it always keep you warm. May we meet again as friends in the pure land of the Buddha.

'May your mind enjoy the serenity of enlightenment. But in your enlightenment do not forget the other living beings in the world. Engender within yourself the urge to bring salvation to all; find within yourself the strength to carry the truth across the world. May we meet again as friends in the pure land of the Buddha.

'My blessed son, I speak to you from the heart. Keep my words in your heart, and do not forget them. I, your mother, shall always remember you. Mother and son, our hearts are one. May we meet again as friends in the pure land of the Buddha.'

Milarepa 2.5

Family, home and land

I left my homeland long ago, in search of a teacher. I leave my homeland again, and return to my teacher; but I find him asleep. Some years later I come back to my homeland.

All that exists is transient, and in constant flux. In this world of change, nothing has purpose or value. Instead of engaging in futile action, I pledge myself to follow the Way.

At first, when my father was ready to teach me, I was not a true son. When I became a true son, my father was no longer with me. So our meetings were illusions.

At first, when my mother was ready to teach me, I was not a true son. When I became a true son, my mother was no longer with me. So our meetings were illusions.

When my sister was ready to teach me, I was not a true brother. When I became a true brother, she had wandered away. So our meetings were illusions.

When I first possessed holy books, I did not venerate them. Now that I venerate them, they are spoiled by rain. So my reading is an illusion.

When I had a house, I was not ready to be a master. Now that I am ready to be a master, I do not have a house. So my house was an illusion.

When I had a field, I could not plough it. Now that I can plough, I do not have a field. So my field was an illusion.

Family, home, land – they belong to the world of illusion. Let the ignorant take them. I seek salvation as a monk, meditating in solitude.

Milarepa 2.6

Worldly things

I have neither the desire to lead a worldly life, nor the ability to be successful in worldly affairs. If I were to try being worldly, I should be like a hare imagining it could follow in the footsteps of a lion.

I am so saddened by the cycle of birth and death, that I wish only to meditate and to obey my teacher's instructions. He taught that meditation should be practised in solitude; and that is what I shall continue to do. Only through meditation can I fulfill his hopes for me. Only through meditation can I help other living beings. My meditation can even save my father and mother – even though they are dead. I only know how to meditate; I can do nothing else.

I have returned to my village because my parents owned a house and a field here. The disappearance of these things has intensified my desire to meditate, which burns like a flame within my breast.

When I think of those who trust in worldly things, I am filled with sadness. Indulging in worldly pleasures reaches down to the very source of misery. The worldly life is one of constant flux; the mind is never still, but lurches in all directions. Those who are trapped by worldly attachments – what can they do? Their only escape is to devote themselves to the Way.

Milarepa 2.6

Examples of transient illusion

My flocks of sheep have been stolen; and the land on which they grazed has been seized by brigands. My house is in ruins; only the corner of a wall still stands, like the ear of a donkey. My sheep, my land, my house – they are examples of transient illusion, which summon me to meditation.

My field, on which crops used to grow, is now overrun by weeds. My cousins, even my close relatives, now regard me as an enemy, and seize my property. My fields, my family – they are examples of transient illusion, which summon me to meditation.

My good father is dead; no trace of him remains. My mother, the jewel of my heart, is nothing but crumbling bones. My father, my mother – they are examples of transient illusion, which summon me to meditation.

The old priest is now reduced to working as a domestic servant in a rich man's house. The holy books, which he used to keep, are now the nests of rats and mice. Priesthood, books – they are examples of transient illusion, which summon me to meditation.

My uncle now lives among my enemies. My sister has wandered, and no one knows where she has gone. My uncle, my sister – they are examples of transient illusion, which summon me to meditation.

Milarepa 2.6

Living as a beggar

My mother has been killed by the arrows of poverty and sorrow. My sister wanders from place to place, begging for food
and clothing. I have never stopped loving my mother and my
sister; so now my heart is sad and bitter.

   Did my cousins plot the fate of my mother and my sister?
Did they intend to overwhelm me with grief? Yet this intolerable grief calls me back to the spiritual life.

   When I last departed from my homeland I lived in a
mountain cave. But my body, though it is a mere illusion,
was wracked with hunger. So I left my cave, and became a
beggar. And I am still a beggar.

   I go to my aunt's house; but she sends a ferocious dog to
welcome me. Despite the weakness of my body, I fight it off.
As I leave, she shouts curses after me; her words pierce my
heart. Then she comes after me, and hits me many times with
a tent pole; as the blows rain down upon me, I nearly die. I
have good cause for resentment against her; but I remain
faithful to the instructions of my teacher.

   Aunt, forget your anger. Give me food to sustain my
body, so I can devote my mind to meditation.

                                                   Milarepa 2.7

A dream of perseverance

My aunt repents. She says that I am a holy man, and promises to cultivate my field, bringing me its harvest.

So I try to meditate. But I cannot attain serenity; I cannot achieve that blissful state of inner warmth that is the fruit of meditation. I wonder what I should do.

Then I have a dream. In my dream I am ploughing a strip of my field. The earth is hard, and I wonder if I should give up. My teacher appears in the sky, and exclaims: 'My son, strengthen your will. Take courage, and work. Soon you will penetrate the hard, dry earth.' So I continue ploughing. Immediately crops spring up, bearing an abundant harvest. I awake full of joy.

At first I think: 'Dreams are nothing more than the expressions of hidden thoughts. Not even fools believe they are real. If I take this dream seriously, I am the biggest fool of all.' But then I find myself taking it seriously. I take it to mean that, if I persevere in my efforts to meditate, I shall attain a higher level of inner experience.

Milarepa 2.7

The soul as a field

My soul is now my field. I turn it with the plough of non-discriminating thought. I fertilize it with the manure of faith. I sow it with the seed of a pure heart. The powerful thunder of my prayers echoes around it; and the rain of divine blessings falls upon it.

The oxen pulling my plough are a mind free of doubt. The yoke is wisdom, and the reins are the absence of distraction. I crack the whip of effort; and the plough breaks up the clods of corrupt emotions. I cast away the stones of anger, and pull up the weeds of hypocrisy. I reap the harvest of love.

I fill the granary with the fruit of truthful teachings; the grain is not defiled by concepts and theories. The angels grind and roast the grain, making it the perfect food for spiritual growth.

Realization is not attained merely through verbal knowledge; understanding does not come from concepts and theories. Those who wish to be enlightened, must practise meditation with perseverance and effort; and with perseverance and effort even the most formidable obstacles will be overcome.

Milarepa 2.7

Anger and greed

I am tortured by the world's continuous state of flux; I yearn to be free from it. Within this continuous state of flux human beings perform evil deeds; and these evil deeds cause them to suffer great misery.

Many people build their lives with the bricks of family loyalty; yet in truth they build a castle of devils, in which a fire constantly rages.

Many people strive to accumulate wealth and riches. Yet sooner or later their possessions are taken by others; everything that a man can acquire, eventually belongs to his enemies or to thieves.

Many people crave tea and beer. Yet to satisfy those cravings is to burst the artery of salvation.

My aunt has acquired my field; if I were to have any part of it, the hungry ghosts of greed would rise again within me. My aunt speaks words of anger; if I were to respond with anger, I should destroy myself – and we should destroy one another.

Aunt, take my house and my field; take them, and may they make you happy. Through my devotion to the Way, you will be released from any blame; and I shall journey to the temple of ultimate truth.

With the weapon of compassion I shall overcome all evil.

Milarepa 2.7

A vow of solitude

Today I have come to the Horse Tooth Rock, without anyone knowing; and I have taken up residence in a pleasant cave. I have brought a mat on which to sit while I meditate. And now I make a vow not to descend to any town or village, to any place where other humans live.

So long as I have not attained spiritual enlightenment, I shall not descend to beg for food – even if I am dying of hunger on this mountain. I shall not descend to beg for clothing – even if I am dying of cold on this mountain. I shall not indulge in any worldly pleasures or amusements – even if I am dying of sadness on this mountain. I shall not descend to seek medicines – even if I am dying of disease on this mountain. In my efforts to become enlightened, I shall not allow myself to be distracted in body, speech or mind.

Teacher, I ask you to bless me, that I may keep this vow. May the angels of the Way support me with their powers. It is better to die, than to live as someone who has broken a vow; it is better to die, than to live as someone who does not strive for truth.

Milarepa 2.7

A prayer for deepening meditation

May I be sheltered from all devils who try to distract me; and may my meditation deepen day by day.

Let the flowers of transcendental intelligence bloom within me; and yet may I not become attached to the lake of my own serenity.

Let the leaves of non-discriminating thought spread across my mind; may no concepts and theories cause them to wither.

Let no doubts inhabit my cell; but may the fruit of inner knowledge ripen. May no devils dare to create spiritual obstacles; may absolute certainty fill my mind.

Let me follow in the footsteps of my teacher, whom I regard as my father; may I never hesitate or stumble.

Milarepa 2.7

The inner fire

I am living on a thin soup, with a little roasted barley. I devote almost every moment to meditation. Yet my body is growing so weak, that I cannot control my breath. And no blissful inner fire warms me, so I shiver with cold.

Then I invoke my teacher, praying to him with great intensity. One night, when my mind is utterly lucid, I have a vision of a great crowd of women, participating in a sacrificial feast. They come towards me, and surround me. And they say: 'Your teacher has sent us to you. He knows that no inner fire warms you. So he has commanded us to instruct you in various techniques of body, mind and soul; and he wants you to practise them until the inner fire is kindled.'

The women demonstrate six bodily postures. I choose one of the postures, known as the six interwoven earths. They show me how to breathe. And they tell me to hold in my mind the image of a snake uncoiling within me. As I practise these techniques, the inner fire begins to burn, and its warmth spreads through me.

Milarepa 2.7

A reminder of the vow

A year passes. I am tempted to leave my cave, and seek to refresh myself elsewhere. Then I recall my vow, and remind myself of it.

I am too proud; let me always remember my vow, and humbly submit to its demands. I have promised to cut myself off from all friends, and to deny myself all conversation.

I look out from my cave over the valley below; but the view is empty, and does not lift my heart. The emptiness of the view is a sign that my mind should be empty of all distractions; no idle thoughts should wander through it. Idle thoughts soon become corrupt thoughts – and then all serenity is lost.

I shall not be distracted. I shall not be distracted. I shall be vigilant and attentive. If I lack vigilance and am inattentive, my devotion will be carried away by the wind.

I shall not leave. I shall not leave. I shall stay where I am. If I leave, my foot will stumble on a stone, and I shall fall.

I shall not seek pleasure, but I shall control myself. Seeking pleasure serves no purpose.

I shall not sleep. I shall not sleep. I shall meditate. If I sleep, corrupt dreams may poison my mind.

Milarepa 2.7

Nettles, sacks and a hunter

Another year passes. My stocks of flour run out. So I go out across the mountains, and collect nettles; these sustain me, but my body turns to their colour.

Another year passes. All my clothes are worn out. The old fur coat, given by my aunt in payment for my field, is in tatters. I wonder about sewing together the empty flour sacks. Then I say to myself: 'If I am to die this evening, it would be wiser to meditate, than to spend my time sewing.' So I spread the tattered fur over my mat, sit down, and pull up the edges to cover the lower parts of my body; and I put some sacks over my shoulders.

Another year passes. A hunter comes past my cave, and sees me. He is astonished at my green skin and emaciated body, and tells me that I am the most wretched and pitiful person on earth. I reply that I am the most fortunate of people, because I have been taught by the finest teacher on earth, and am now striving to reach eternity. I tell him that there is no person braver than I am, and no one with higher aspirations than I have. I explain to him that his life, in which he piles one sin upon another, is far more dangerous than living alone on a mountain; whereas he suffers continuous disturbance, I enjoy serenity – and am assured that I shall soon enjoy supreme bliss.

Milarepa 2.7

A song of happiness

I sing a song of happiness to the hunter.

I, a Tibetan monk, have renounced food and clothing, in order to become perfectly enlightened.

I am happy with the hard mat beneath me. I am happy with the rough sacks that cover me. I am happy with the cord of meditation which is tied around my knees. I am happy with my body, which is neither starved nor satiated – and which in truth is a mere illusion. I am happy with my soul, which has gained spiritual insight. I am not unhappy; I am happy.

If it seems to you that I am happy, then do as I have done. You may say that you are not religious. But consider only the question of happiness. Consider your happiness, and consider my happiness. Which happiness is real and lasting? Of all beings, do not take pity on me.

The sun is now setting, so return to your home. Life is short, and death strikes without warning. So I have no more time for useless words; leave me to my meditation.

Milarepa 2.7

Words of hope

The hunter returns to his home. Later at a festival he sings my song of happiness; and my sister, who is begging at the festival, hears the song, and knows at once that I composed it. The hunter directs her to my cave. When she sees me, she faints. I am both joyful and sad to see her. When she has regained consciousness, she puts her head on my knees, and sobs. Then I sing her a song.

O sister, all joys and pains are ephemeral. I promise that lasting happiness is possible. We had parents, who are now dead; and their passing grieves you. Yet all living beings are our parents.

This cave is no better than a lair for savage beasts; and many would be indignant that a human being should live in such a place. Yet it is the perfect place for spiritual work.

My food is like the food of dogs and swine; at the sight of it many would be overcome with nausea. My body is like a skeleton; at the sight of it even an enemy would weep. My behaviour is like that of a lunatic; even you, my sister, blush with shame.

But my knowledge is deep and my wisdom profound; spiritual victory will be mine. My body is green, like the nettles I consume; but my heart is bright. By the power of my meditation I shall attain enlightenment – and then my happiness will be complete.

Milarepa 2.7

Wishing for obscurity

The following day my sister leaves. Then several days later she returns with the hunter, who brings food and clothing for me. I tell them that I do not want food and clothing. My sister remonstrates with me, saying that my present condition is miserable. I reply with a song.

My spiritual happiness is unknown to my own sister. My physical misery is unknown to my enemies. I shall die in solitude; that is all I want.

My growing old will be unknown to my friends. My growing sick will be unknown to my sister. I shall die in solitude; that is all I want.

My dying will be unknown to all. My rotting corpse will be unseen by vultures. I shall die in solitude; that is all I want.

There will be no vigil around my corpse. There will be no grief over my death. I shall die in solitude; that is all I want.

No one will speak of my life. No one will regret its end. I shall die in solitude; that is all I want.

Let this cave in the mountain be my grave. Yet I live, and I shall die, for the sake of every living being.

                                                        Milarepa 2.7

The soul as a horse

Think of my soul as a horse which flies like the wind.

If I want to catch him, what kind of lasso shall I use? If I want to tie him, what kind of stake shall I use? If he is hungry, with what kind of fodder shall I feed him? If he is thirsty, where shall I find water? If he is cold, with what wall shall I shelter him?

If I catch him, it will be with the lasso of unconditional love. If I tie him, it will be with the stake of deep meditation. If I feed him, it will be with the instructions of enlightened teachers. If I give him drink, it will be with water from the perpetual stream of vigilance. If I shelter him, it will be with the walls of emptiness.

For saddle and bit, I shall use knowledge and wisdom. For reins I shall use spiritual vitality. The child of insight will ride him. For a helmet he will wear enlightenment. His coat of mail will be fashioned from listening and questioning. On his breast he will wear the armour of patience. At his side will be fastened the sword of intuition.

His arrow will be pure consciousness. If it bends, he will straighten it without anger. He will let loose his arrows across the world. They will strike those who have faith – and they will slay the self.

His enemy is desire and delusion. He gallops towards the land of pure bliss. Sometimes he goes backwards, and cuts the roots of flux. And as he goes forward, the light of truth guides him.

Milarepa 2.7

True and false shame

My sister is ashamed of my nakedness. She asks me to ensure that my sexual organ is always covered. I make a garment for my lower body; yet I tell her that every part of the body is equal. Then I sing about shame.

You, virgin sister, are bound by foolish modesty. Ignorance causes you to blush at things that are not shameful. But I, a monk, understand what shame really is. If we live virtuously in body, speech and mind, why should shame arise?

The differences between men and women are clear to everyone. Yet true modesty and decency are rare. The man who marries the woman with the greatest dowry – he should feel shame. The woman who regards her child as her own possession – she should feel shame.

Greed and hatred, robbery and fraud, the betrayal of friends – these are truly shameful. And few are innocent of them. They arise from distortions in the mind.

Monks, who have renounced the world, devote themselves to the Way. They have no cause for shame. So, dear sister, your shame at my nakedness is false; and the antidote to false shame is purity of mind.

Milarepa 2.7

Teaching from experience

My sister and the hunter spread news of me; and people flock to become my disciples. Since I have never studied logic, I teach them only from my own experience.

The instructions of my own teacher penetrated my thoughts, and drove out all distractions.

I meditated on love and compassion; and the distinction between myself and others disappeared from my mind.

I meditated on my teacher; and the distinction between those who are powerful and influential, and those who are weak and oppressed, disappeared from my mind.

I meditated constantly on divinity; and the coarse world of the senses disappeared from my mind.

I meditated on pure awareness; and the illusions of ignorance disappeared from my mind.

I meditated on this life and the life beyond; and the fear of birth and death disappeared from my mind.

I meditated on the joys of solitude; and the need to please my relatives and my friends disappeared from my mind.

Milarepa 2.9

The spirit not the letter

I assimilated the instructions of my teacher into the stream of my consciousness; all urge to engage in doctrinal argument disappeared from my mind.

I meditated on that which has no origin, which has no end, and which does not abide; and all conventional forms disappeared from my mind.

I meditated on external objects as figments of the mind; and all concepts disappeared from my mind.

I lived in a manner that was entirely natural; and all temptation to hypocrisy disappeared from my mind.

I lived in a manner that was humble in body, speech and mind; and all desire for status disappeared from my mind.

I made my own body my community; and the monastic community outside disappeared from my mind.

I embraced the spirit, rather than the letter, of all that I had learnt; and the ability to play with words disappeared from my mind.

Milarepa 2.9

Sin and purity

Owing to your past lives, you have taken pleasure in evil since the day you were born. Throughout childhood you had no yearning for virtue. And now in adulthood your minds are impure.

Do you ask whether you may be purified from sin? If you ask that question, it is a sign that you wish to be purified from sin; and the wish will bring its own fulfilment. Do you knowingly commit evil acts? If you do, then any material profit is gained at the price of guilt and shame.

Do not pose as a teacher of others, while you remain ignorant of the truth yourself. False teachers harm themselves, as well as those they instruct.

If you sincerely wish to avoid all suffering, then avoid any action that will cause suffering to others. If you sincerely wish to be free from guilt, repent of the times in the past when you caused suffering to others. Vow never to harm others again; then, if you keep that vow, you will become pure.

Most sinners are clever. They aim low with great accuracy. If they have no spiritual impulse, this shows that their minds are utterly polluted.

Strive without ceasing for purity. Dispel ignorance, and accumulate merit. Eventually you will come to discern divinity within yourself. At that time you will see the whole truth of flux and of nirvana.

Milarepa 2.9

Prayers for the future

My disciples, you have been kind to me; and I have felt great love for you. May we meet again as friends in the pure land of the Buddha. In the meantime may all of you have long and happy lives. May your spiritual aspirations be fulfilled, without being hindered by harmful thoughts.

May this region be blessed. May it be free from disease and war, and may it enjoy rich harvests. And may my disciples always devote themselves to the Way. May we meet again as friends in the pure land of the Buddha.

All of you who have seen and heard me, who have listened to my story, and who remember all that I have said – you are my friends. All of you who venerate me, who pass on to others what I have said, and who strive to follow my example – you are my friends. May we meet again as friends in the pure land of the Buddha.

Let men and women in the future meditate as I have done, and practise the asceticism that I have practised. May every obstacle be swept aside, and every error corrected.

May those who practise asceticism, be richly blessed, gathering an abundant harvest of merit. May those who help others to practise asceticism, be greatly honoured, receiving abundant gratitude from all.

May those who meditate in a cave, as I have done, and dress in sacks, as I have done, enjoy immeasurable bliss.

Milarepa 2.9

What benefit?

Without having an enlightened teacher, what benefit is there in being initiated as a disciple?

Without inner awareness of the Way, what benefit is there in learning sacred texts by heart?

Without renouncing worldly aims and ambitions, what benefit is there in meditating?

Without attuning your body, speech and mind to the Way, what benefit is there in religious ceremonies?

If you cannot tolerate an insult, what benefit is there in meditating on patience?

If you cannot overcome both attachment and revulsion, what benefit is there in helping the poor?

If you cannot rid yourself of all selfishness, what benefit is there in becoming leader of a great monastery?

If faith does not grow within your mind, what benefit is there in building temples and shrines?

If you do not follow my instructions, what good is there in mourning my death?

                                                    Milarepa 2.9

Pray as one

If you do not follow my instructions, your meditation will lead you astray. If you do not follow my instructions, your asceticism will torment you.

Those who do not subdue desire and banish illusion, only speak empty and futile words. Those who have not learnt the art of meditation, will fail to meditate, however hard they try. Those who have not acquired the key to the entrance, can never follow the Way, however great their determination. Those who do not give up their possessions for the sake of the truth, will never attain perfection, however much they yearn for it.

Material desire provokes rivalry between friends. Desire for status provokes resentment between friends. Keeping silent about oneself prevents conflict. Solitude is the ideal companion. Humility is the highest goal.

Realization of emptiness evokes compassion. And compassion dissolves the differences between people. When there is duality between one person and another, happiness comes. Those who care about the needs of others, care about knowledge; and they will attain enlightenment.

You are all one. Think of yourselves as one. Pray as one. Those are my final words; I have nothing further to say. I shall pass into nirvana.

Milarepa 2.9

Ten evils

If you seek salvation and perfect wisdom, you should beware ten evils.

The first. Having received a human body, do not fritter life away.

The second. Having received a human body, do not die as a worldly person.

The third. Since this life is so brief and uncertain, do not spend it on pursuing worldly aims and goals.

The fourth. Since the soul can apprehend the truth, do not swallow up the mind in worldly illusions.

The fifth. Since there are enlightened teachers who can offer guidance on the Way, do not ignore these teachers.

The sixth. Since religious faith is the vessel which conveys the soul to salvation, do not shatter faith with uncontrolled passions.

The seventh. Since perfect wisdom is to be found within the soul, do not lose wisdom in the jungle of worldly anxieties.

The eighth. Do not teach the Way in exchange for worldly wealth.

The ninth. Since birth and rebirth have been continuing for countless aeons, and since therefore every living being has once been parent to every other living being, do not dislike or mistreat any living being.

The tenth. Since youth is the period in which the body and the mind develop, do not waste it in indolence and indifference.

Dvagpo-Lharje 1

Ten requirements

If you seek salvation and perfect wisdom, you should fulfill ten requirements.

The first. Having estimated your capabilities, take a clear line of action.

The second. In carrying out the instructions of your teacher, be confident and determined.

The third. In choosing a teacher, assess every possible teacher's faults and virtues.

The fourth. In understanding your teacher's instructions, apply both your intellect and your intuition.

The fifth. In order to keep your body, speech and mind unsullied by evil, be vigilant, alert, and humble.

The sixth. In fulfilling your highest aspirations, wear spiritual armour.

The seventh. To free yourself from bondage, suppress desire and attachment.

The eighth. In order to acquire both temporal and spiritual merit, ensure that you have the right motives, and perform the right actions.

The ninth. In order to develop the right motives and perform the right actions, ensure that you have love and compassion for all living beings.

The tenth. In order not to fall into the error of imagining that external objects are real, strive to understand the true nature of all existence.

Dvagpo-Lharje 2

Ten things to be done

If you seek salvation and perfect wisdom, you should realize there are ten things to be done.

The first. Attach yourself to a spiritual teacher endowed with spiritual power and profound knowledge.

The second. Live where there are benign psychic influences.

The third. Seek friends whose aims and methods are similar to your own, in whom you can put your trust.

The fourth. Eat only just enough to keep yourself healthy.

The fifth. Study the writings of all the religions and sects, with an open and impartial mind.

The sixth. Study the precious sciences of medicine and astrology, and become proficient in the profound art of omens.

The seventh. Adopt a daily pattern of life which is healthy.

The eighth. Perform such rituals, and recite such prayers, as may be helpful to your spiritual development.

The ninth. Accept as disciples those who are firm in faith and meek in spirit, and who appear to be ready to seek divine wisdom.

The tenth. When you are walking or sitting, and when you are eating or sleeping, always be aware of what you are doing.

Dvagpo-Lharje 3

Ten things to be avoided

If you seek salvation and perfect wisdom, you should avoid ten things.

The first. Avoid a teacher whose heart is set on worldly fame and wealth.

The second. Avoid friends and disciples who upset your peace of mind and hinder your spiritual development.

The third. Avoid living in places where there are many neighbours who are liable to annoy or distract you.

The fourth. Avoid gaining your livelihood by means of deceit and theft.

The fifth. Avoid any actions which may upset your peace of mind and hinder your spiritual development.

The sixth. Avoid rowdy or thoughtless behaviour which will reduce other people's respect for you.

The seventh. Avoid wasting your time with worthless activities.

The eighth. Avoid concealing your own faults, and drawing attention to the faults of others.

The ninth. Avoid any foods, and break any habits, which damage your health.

The tenth. Avoid any attachments which arise from greed.

Dvagpo-Lharje 4

Ten things not to avoid

If you seek salvation and perfect wisdom, you should not avoid ten things.

The first. Do not avoid ideas, since ideas are light to the mind.

The second. Do not avoid thinking, since thinking is the means of playing with the truth.

The third. Do not avoid being honest about your emotions, since honesty about your emotions enables you to control them.

The fourth. Do not avoid simple comforts, since they are like manure for spiritual growth.

The fifth. Do not avoid illness and distress, since these are teachers of piety.

The sixth. Do not avoid enemies, since they remind you of why you have chosen to pursue spiritual goals.

The seventh. Do not avoid that which cannot be avoided, since that which cannot be avoided is a divine gift.

The eighth. Do not avoid rationality, since in all situations rationality is your best friend.

The ninth. Do not avoid exercises of body and mind which maintain your health.

The tenth. Do not avoid planning how to help others.

Dvagpo-Lharje 5

Ten things to know

If you seek salvation and perfect wisdom, you should know ten things.

The first. Know that all visible phenomena are illusory and unreal.

The second. Know that the soul is dependent on the universal soul.

The third. Know that ideas arise from the coincidence of disparate perceptions.

The fourth. Know that body and speech are transient.

The fifth. Know that the consequences of past actions are unavoidable.

The sixth. Know that sorrow reminds you of the need for leading the spiritual life.

The seventh. Know that attachment to material things is contrary to spiritual progress.

The eighth. Know that misfortune is a teacher.

The ninth. Know that no living being exists independently.

The tenth. Know that all living beings are interdependent.

Dvagpo-Lharje 6

Ten things to be practised

If you seek salvation and perfect wisdom, you should practise ten things.

The first. Acquire practical knowledge of the spiritual path you are treading.

The second. Acquire practical knowledge of non-attachment.

The third. Separate yourself from all sense of self.

The fourth. Regard yourself as subservient to the truth, never boasting of your spiritual attainments.

The fifth. Cultivate spiritual knowledge with ceaseless vigilance, never neglecting it through indolence.

The sixth. Having once experienced spiritual insight, reflect on that insight in solitude.

The seventh. Take three vows, of poverty, of chastity, and of obedience to your teacher; and observe those vows in body, speech and mind.

The eighth. Devote yourself to the service of others, never acting selfishly.

The ninth. Cherish holiness in body, speech and mind.

The tenth. Undertake no spiritual practice, except on the instruction of a wise and pious teacher.

Dvagpo-Lharje 7

Ten things to be persevered in

If you seek salvation and perfect wisdom, you should persevere in ten things.

The first. Persevere in listening to, and reflecting upon, wise spiritual teachings.

The second. Persevere in meditation and in mental concentration.

The third. Persevere in solitude, until your mind is fully controlled.

The fourth. When thoughts are difficult to control, persevere in your efforts to dominate them.

The fifth. When you feel drowsy, persevere in your efforts to invigorate the mind.

The sixth. Persevere in your spiritual discipline until you have attained mental serenity.

The seventh. Having attained mental serenity, persevere in maintaining it and ensuring that it recurs.

The eighth. When misfortune befalls you, persevere in patience of body, speech and mind.

The ninth. When you find yourself hankering for some material thing, and your mind feels weak, persevere in your efforts to suppress the hankering.

The tenth. If love and compassion grow cold within you, persevere in rekindling them.

Dvagpo-Lharje 8

Ten motives

If you seek salvation and perfect wisdom, motivate yourself in ten ways.

The first. Reflect on the benefits to the body's health of the spiritual life.

The second. Reflect on death and the impermanence of life.

The third. Reflect on the good consequences of good actions, and the evil consequences of evil actions.

The fourth. Reflect on the many evils you have suffered though countless previous lives, and hence yearn for freedom from birth and rebirth.

The fifth. Reflect on the miseries which all living beings suffer, and hence yearn for their freedom from suffering.

The sixth. Reflect on the illusory nature of all external things.

The seventh. Reflect on the difficulty of eradicating errors from the mind, and hence strive harder in doing so.

The eighth. Reflect on the stubbornness of evil propensities and desires, and hence strive harder to eradicate them.

The ninth. Reflect on the uncertainty of life, remembering that misfortune may strike at any time.

The tenth. Reflect on the dissatisfaction of frittering your life away, and hence renew your sense of purpose.

Dvagpo-Lharje 9

Ten errors

If you seek salvation and perfect wisdom, you should beware ten errors.

The first. Do not combine weakness of faith with strength of intellect, as this would make you talkative.

The second. Do not combine strength of faith with weakness of intellect, as this would make you narrow-minded and dogmatic.

The third. Do not combine religious zeal with lack of spiritual guidance, as this would make you go to harmful extremes.

The fourth. Do not meditate without pondering on the Way, as this would lead to mental chaos.

The fifth. Do not reject rationality, as this would lead to self-delusion.

The sixth. Do not seek salvation for yourself alone, as this would be self-defeating.

The seventh. Do not pursue worldly wealth, as this would make you imagine that external things are real.

The eighth. Do not pursue worldly ambition, as this would make you imagine that external status is real.

The ninth. Do not let people admire you, as this would puff you up with pride.

The tenth. Do not boast of your psychic powers, as this would make people admire you.

Dvagpo-Lharje 10

Ten mistakes

If you seek salvation and perfect wisdom, you should beware ten mistakes.

The first. Do not mistake the desire for spiritual perfection for genuine faith.

The second. Do not mistake attachment to worthwhile objects for genuine benevolence.

The third. Do not mistake the cessation of thought for serenity of mind.

The fourth. Do not mistake perceptions of phenomena with understanding of them.

The fifth. Do not mistake glimpses of reality with complete realization.

The sixth. Do not mistake those who outwardly profess religious faith, with those who put faith into practice.

The seventh. Do not mistake those who flout convention out of passion, with those who flout convention out of spiritual salvation.

The eighth. Do not mistake acts of self-interest with acts of altruism.

The ninth. Do not mistake clever spiritual methods with wise spiritual methods.

The tenth. Do not mistake charlatans with genuine spiritual sages.

Dvagpo-Lharje 11

Ten ways of avoiding mistakes

If you seek salvation and perfect wisdom, observe these ten ways of avoiding mistakes.

The first. Give up your home, as your home is your strongest attachment.

The second. Revere your spiritual teacher.

The third. Study the spiritual writings about the Way, and listen to discourses about the Way, reflecting on what you read and hear.

The fourth. Have lofty aspirations, and a lowly demeanour.

The fifth. Be open-minded and tolerant on religious matters, and yet firm in your spiritual commitment.

The sixth. Expand your intellect, and diminish your pride.

The seventh. Become rich in spiritual knowledge, and diligent in meditating on this wealth.

The eighth. Take every opportunity to learn more about spiritual matters.

The ninth. Learn to prefer solitude to company.

The tenth. Be kind to others, and choose the most effective methods of exercising kindness.

Dvagpo-Lharje 12

If you seek salvation and perfect wisdom, you should beware ten failures.

The first. If, having been taught the truth, you do not follow it, you are like someone returning empty-handed from a land rich in precious gems.

The second. If, having become a monk, you return to the life of a householder, you are like a moth flying into a flame.

The third. If you live with a wise teacher, and yet remain ignorant, you are like someone dying of thirst on the shore of a lake.

The fourth. If you flout the moral precepts you have been given, you are like a sick person who refuses to take medicine.

The fifth. If you preach religion, but do not practise it, you are like a parrot.

The sixth. If you give to the poor money which you have obtained by robbery and deceit, you are like lightning striking the surface of water.

The seventh. If you pretend to be patient, you are like a cat stalking a mouse.

The eighth. If you do good merely to obtain respect, you are exchanging a precious gem for a piece of goat's dung.

The ninth. If you are clever in expounding religion, but have had no spiritual experiences, you are like a rich man who has lost the key to his treasury.

The tenth. If you try to explain teachings which you do not understand yourself, you are like a blind man leading the blind.

Dvagpo-Lharje 13

Ten weaknesses

If you seek salvation and perfect wisdom, you should beware ten weaknesses.

The first. When living in solitude, do not fill your mind with worldly thoughts.

The second. When heading a monastery, do not further your own interests.

The third. When following the spiritual path, do not cling to feelings of attraction and repulsion.

The fourth. Do not become a monk in order to gain merit.

The fifth. Do not be content with just a glimpse of reality; be satisfied only when realization is complete.

The sixth. Do not worry about where you will obtain food and clothing.

The seventh. Do not praise yourself, while disparaging others.

The eighth. Do not preach higher standards to others than you yourself practise.

The ninth. If you cannot live in solitude, but must live in company, do not make yourself disagreeable to others.

The tenth. Do not discriminate between comfort and hardship.

Dvagpo-Lharje 14

Ten indispensable things

If you seek salvation and perfect wisdom, you require ten indispensable things.

The first. Have a profound aversion to the interminable sequence of birth, death and rebirth.

The second. Have a teacher who has trodden the spiritual path.

The third. Have determination to resist temptation.

The fourth. Have determination to neutralize the consequences of evil deeds, by performing good deeds.

The fifth. Have a philosophy capable of embracing the whole of knowledge.

The sixth. Have a method of meditating that will concentrate the mind.

The seventh. Have a way of life which is healthy for every part of the body.

The eighth. Have a way of selecting those teachings which are useful to you at present, and ignoring those teachings that will become useful later.

The ninth. Have serenity at the prospect of death.

The tenth. Have a method of perceiving the divine essence within yourself.

Dvagpo-Lharje 15

Ten signs of superiority

If you seek salvation and perfect wisdom, you should know ten signs of superiority.

The first. To have little pride and no envy.

The second. To have few desires, and to be satisfied with simple things.

The third. To have no hypocrisy and deceit.

The fourth. To regulate your conduct, recognizing that every action has a consequence.

The fifth. To fulfill your duties to others, and to keep your promises.

The sixth. To maintain friendships, while at the same time being impartial between one person and another.

The seventh. To look with pity rather than anger towards those who do evil.

The eighth. In any conflict or dispute to allow others to be victorious, and take defeat on yourself.

The ninth. To be willing to differ from common opinion in your views, and to flout convention in your actions.

The tenth. To observe your vows of poverty, chastity and obedience; and yet to take no pride in doing so.

Dvagpo-Lharje 16

Ten useless things

If you seek salvation and perfect wisdom, you need to beware ten useless things.

The first. Since the body is illusory and transient, do not pay it undue attention.

The second. Since at death you will take nothing with you, do not labour hard to accumulate wealth.

The third. Since at death your relatives cannot assist you, do not try to win their love with material gifts.

The fourth. Since you make the journey of death alone, do not try to win favour with relatives and friends by humouring them.

The fifth. Since every bequest is eventually lost, do not aim to bequeath any wealth.

The sixth. Since in death you must relinquish your own home, do not strive to build yourself anything grand.

The seventh. Do not become a monk if you do not intend to become holy.

The eighth. Since psychic powers bring no benefit at death, do not seek to acquire them.

The ninth. Do not become a monk, if you are not sufficiently humble to obey a teacher.

The tenth. Since the external world is neither real nor permanent, do not regard anything as your own.

Dvagpo-Lharje 17

Ten self-imposed troubles

If you seek salvation and perfect wisdom, you should beware ten self-imposed troubles.

The first. Do not stay in someone's house, unless you can pay them for your lodging.

The second. Do not behave maliciously, as malice engenders moral insanity.

The third. Do not be hypocritical, as hypocrisy poisons your own mind.

The fourth. Do not put yourself forward as leader of a monastery, if your mind is weak; you would be like an old woman trying to herd cattle.

The fifth. Do not strive for your own good, without striving equally for the good of others; you would be like a blind man wandering into the desert.

The sixth. Do not undertake tasks which are beyond your capacity or ability.

The seventh. Do not allow pride or conceit to induce you to flout your teacher's instructions; you would be like a king ignoring his advisers.

The eighth. Do not loiter unnecessarily in towns and villages; you would be like a deer feeding in the valley, instead of remaining secure on the mountain.

The ninth. Do not pursue worldly wisdom in preference to spiritual wisdom; you would be like an eagle deliberately breaking its own wing.

The tenth. Do not use for yourself offerings which have been made to your teacher; that would be like a child swallowing hot coals.

Dvagpo-Lharje 18

Ten ways of doing good to yourself

If you seek salvation and perfect wisdom, you do yourself good in ten ways.

The first. Abandon worldly conventions, and devote yourself to the Way.

The second. Depart from home and family, and attach yourself to a teacher of saintly character.

The third. Relinquish worldly concerns and activities, and spend your time listening to, reflecting upon, and meditating on wise teachings.

The fourth. Give up social intercourse, and live in solitude.

The fifth. Renounce desire for luxury and comfort, and learn to endure hardship.

The sixth. Be content with simple things.

The seventh. Never take advantage of others.

The eighth. Suppress all hankering after transient pleasures, and seek only eternal happiness.

The ninth. Remind yourself constantly that visible and tangible things are unreal and illusory.

The tenth. Ensure that you know only what you should know, by controlling what you do, hear, and think.

Dvagpo-Lharje 19

Ten equal things

If you seek salvation and perfect peace, you should regard ten things as equal.

The first. When you are firm in your faith, it is the same whether you refrain from worldly activities or engage in them.

The second. When you have attained realization, it is the same whether you meditate or not.

The third. When you have freed yourself from worldly attachments, it is the same whether you practise asceticism or not.

The fourth. When you know reality, it is the same whether you live in solitude on a mountain or not.

The fifth. When you have gained mastery over the mind, it is the same whether you live in solitude on a mountain or not.

The sixth. When you love, it is the same whether you do good or not.

The seventh. When you are truly humble, it is the same whether you live with a teacher or not.

The eighth. When you understand the teachings you have received, it is the same whether good fortune or bad fortune befalls you.

The ninth. For a monk, abiding by conventions or flouting them is the same.

The tenth. When you are truly wise, it is the same whether you exercise miraculous powers or not.

Dvagpo-Lharje 25

Ten figurative expressions

If you seek salvation and perfect wisdom, you should regard ten expressions as figurative.

The first. In spiritual matters 'truth' is figurative.

The second. In the phrase 'spiritual path', 'path' is figurative.

The third. In spiritual matters 'seeing' is figurative.

The fourth. In regard to meditation and morality, the word 'purity' is figurative.

The fifth. In regard to the fruits of meditation, the term 'bliss' is figurative, since in a state of serenity there can be no feelings.

The sixth. In the spiritual life the term 'vow' is figurative, because 'vow' implies the existence of an independent will.

The seventh. The term 'accumulating merit' is figurative, since merit is not a substance which can be heaped up.

The eighth. The term 'action' is figurative, because all action is illusory.

The ninth. The phrase 'renouncing the world' is figurative, since the world is illusory, and therefore cannot be renounced.

The tenth. For the same reason 'consequences of actions' is figurative.

Dvagpo-Lharje 27

Ten joyful realizations

If you seek salvation and perfect wisdom, you should anticipate ten joyful realizations.

The first. Realizing that the souls of all living beings are inseparable from the universal soul.

The second. Realizing that in truth there are no differences in quality.

The third. Realizing that thought can be transcended.

The fourth. Realizing that, when thought has been transcended, nothing can disturb the mind.

The fifth. Realizing that matter is mind.

The sixth. Realizing that birth, death and rebirth can cease.

The seventh. Realizing that there is duality between the subject which knows, and the object which is known.

The eighth. Realizing that theological theories are empty of meaning.

The ninth. Realizing that compassion has no bounds and is impartial.

The tenth. Realizing that the path to salvation always exists, and is open to all.

Dvagpo-Lharje 28

ZEN MYSTICISM

The term 'Zen' is derived from an ancient Indian word, meaning 'meditation'. The Zen form of Buddhism began in the sixth century CE in China, and spread to Japan. Its most striking aspect is its method of teaching: it uses stories, jokes and aphorisms which defy reason and logic, and transcend all normal categories of thought. The Zen teachers derived much of their inspiration from earlier Mahayana works, most notably the *Diamond Sutra* and the *Lankavatara Sutra*.

The first major Zen teacher, whose work has been preserved, was Hui-neng (d. 713). The story of his own enlightenment exemplifies the Zen method; and based on his experience, he taught that enlightenment can be attained in an instant.

In the following century Linji (d. 867) founded a school of Zen which was based on Hui-neng's method. It became known as the 'Sudden School'; and Linji is commonly regarded as the greatest of all Zen teachers.

In the eleventh century Setcho (d. 1052) made a collection of a hundred stories of earlier teachers, adding his own commentary. A similar collection was made two centuries later by Mumon (d. 1260).

Coming to Tung-shan monastery

My father was dismissed from his post as a government official, and forced to work as a labourer. He died when I was very young, leaving my mother poor and wretched. In due course I earned money selling firewood in the market.

One day a customer asked me to carry firewood to his shop. When I came out of the shop, I heard a man reciting a spiritual text. As I heard the words of the text, my mind at once was awakened. I asked the man the name of the text; and he told me it was the *Diamond Sutra*. I then asked him where he had heard it. He replied that he came from the Tung-shan monastery, where the abbot, Hung-jen, taught it to both monks and laity.

The merit which I had earned in former lives, was the reason why I heard about this monastery. It was also the reason why a man then gave me enough money to support my mother, and urged me to go to the monastery myself. It took me a month to travel there.

At once I went to pay homage to the abbot. He said to me: 'You are uneducated. How can you expect to attain enlightenment?' I replied: 'Education is not relevant to enlightenment.' The abbot said: 'You are too clever. Go and work in the kitchen, and do not speak any more.'

Hui-neng 1

Transmitting the Way

The next day the abbot came secretly to see me, and found me pounding rice with a stone pestle and mortar. He said to me: 'Seekers of truth risk their lives for the Way. Is this not right?' Then he added: 'Is the rice ready?' I replied: 'It was ready long ago. I was only waiting for a sieve.' He knocked the mortar three times with his stick, and left.

I understood this message; and in the third quarter of the night I went to his cell. He expounded the *Diamond Sutra* to me; and at once I could see that all things in the universe are figments of the mind. I said to the abbot: 'Who would have thought that the soul is essentially pure? Who would have thought that the soul is self-sufficient? Who would have thought that the soul is free from change? Who would have thought that all things are figments of the mind?'

Realizing that I understood the soul, the abbot said: 'Religion is useless to those who do not know their own souls. But those who do know their own souls, are heroes.'

Thus in the middle of the night, with no one else aware of what was happening, the Way was transmitted to me. I received the robe and the begging bowl of a monk.

Hui-neng 1

Thinking of neither good nor evil

I left the Tung-shan monastery, and walked south; after two months I reached Ta-yu mountain. I was pursued by a group of men intent on stealing my robe and begging bowl. Their leader was a monk called Hui-ming, who had a rude manner and a hot temper. When he was about to overtake me, I threw down my robe and begging bowl, exclaiming: 'The robe is nothing but a symbol.'

Hui-ming tried to pick them up; but he found himself unable to do so. Then he said to me: 'I come for the Way, not the robe.' Then he knelt down in front of me.

I said to him: 'If you really come for the Way, not the robe, then make your mind blank. Stop thinking of anything. Once your thoughts have stopped, I shall teach you.' After some time I asked: 'When you are thinking of neither good nor evil, what appears to be your real nature?'

As soon as I asked this question, he became enlightened.

Hui-neng 1

Becoming a teacher

I then went to Szu-hui, where I stayed with a group of hunters for fifteen years. I used to watch the traps which they laid; and whenever an animal was caught, I set it free. I also cooked many of their meals, and used vegetables instead of meat.

Eventually I thought that I should not remain in seclusion any longer, and should teach the Way. So I went to the temple in Canton. One day in the temple, when a pennant was blowing in the wind, two monks began to quarrel about whether the motion was in the wind or in the pennant. I intervened, saying that the motion was in neither, and that the motion was in their minds. All the monks in the temple were astonished at my words.

The abbot invited me to take the seat of honour, and questioned me about various difficult religious points. My answers were so precise and profound, that he said: 'Tell us about the Way and about salvation.' I replied: 'I cannot tell you both about the Way and about salvation.' 'Why not?' he asked. I said: 'If I could tell you both about the Way and about salvation, that would mean there were two aspects of truth. But there can only be one truth.'

The abbot was delighted with my answer, and put his palms together as a sign of respect. Then he asked me to accept him as a pupil. Subsequently I gave many lectures at that temple.

Hui-neng 1

The presence of perfect wisdom in all beings

Good people, perfect wisdom is already present in every living being. Since your minds are deluded, you fail to realize this; so you have to seek the guidance of teachers who do — teachers who have realized the perfect wisdom. As regards the presence of perfect wisdom, there is no difference between an enlightened person and an ignorant person. The difference is that enlightened people realize perfect wisdom within them, whereas ignorant people do not realize it.

Good people, those who talk about perfect wisdom all day long, do not realize that they already possess it. Just as talking about food does not satisfy hunger, so talking about perfect wisdom does not lead to enlightenment. Rather than talk about perfect wisdom, you must put it into practice; indeed, merely talking about wisdom can strengthen the delusion of the mind.

Perfect wisdom is as great as all space. It is infinite. It is neither round nor square, neither great nor small, neither green nor yellow, neither red nor white, neither above nor below, neither long nor short, neither good nor evil, neither first nor last. Perfect wisdom is emptiness; and it is the fullness of emptiness.

Hui-neng 2

Prejudices and errors

Good people, perfect wisdom, which is present in the souls of all living beings, may be compared with rain: the moisture of rain refreshes every plant and tree, every animal and human. Perfect wisdom may be compared with rivers and streams: they all eventually reach the sea, where they merge into a single entity.

When rain pours from the sky in a great deluge, plants with shallow roots are washed away, and eventually die. When the Way is taught to people with shallow thoughts, they too perish. They already possess perfect wisdom, to the same degree as people with deep thoughts; but they will not allow themselves to be enlightened.

When thick clouds cover the sky, the light of the sun cannot reach the earth; but when the clouds are blown away, the sun's brightness shines everywhere. The thoughts of many people are clouded by prejudices and errors, which prevent enlightenment from reaching them. But when these prejudices and errors are blown away, they will attain enlightenment.

Perfect wisdom does not vary from one person to another. People only differ as to whether they are enlightened or deluded. Those who are deluded, believe they can realize perfect wisdom through performing religious rituals. But those who are enlightened, attach no importance to rituals. They know that freedom from prejudices and errors is the condition for realizing perfect wisdom.

Hui-neng 2

The body as a city

Good people, the body may be compared with a city. The eyes, ears, nose and tongue are the gates. The mind is the land on which the city is built. The soul is the king who rules the city. When the mind is away, the body decays.

You should strive for enlightenment of the mind. You should not look for enlightenment outside yourselves, but within yourselves. Most people remain ignorant of the mind. But those who understand and know the mind, are enlightened.

Those who are enlightened are compassionate and merciful; they take delight in serving others. Those who are enlightened, are competent; their service of others does great good. Those who are enlightened regard all people as equal, and are totally honest.

When enlightenment is attained, a pure light emanates from the mind, illuminating the gates of the city, and purifying them. This pure light drives away all evil which may try to enter the city. It also purifies the city itself. So the entire city is free from all sin.

Do you not wish to attain enlightenment?

Hui-neng 3

The spirits of pure minds

For a pure mind moral rules are unnecessary. For an enlightened mind spiritual disciplines are superfluous.

In a spirit of gratitude, those with pure minds support their parents, and treat them with honour. In a spirit of justice, those with pure minds use their wealth to care for the poor, so that in times of famine they eat no more than their poorest neighbours. In a spirit of affection, those with pure minds are courteous to everyone, regarding no one with contempt or disdain. In a spirit of forbearance, those with pure minds never quarrel, even with those who are hostile towards them.

If you persevere, fire can be kindled by rubbing a piece of wood. In the same way, if you persevere, the fire of enlightenment can be kindled by contemplating truth.

Good medicine tastes bitter. In the same way, frank advice is often unpleasant to the ear. By taking frank advice, wisdom is acquired; by resisting frank advice out of pride, ignorance is maintained.

In daily life altruism should always be practised. But acts of charity do not lead to enlightenment. The path to enlightenment is within the mind. There is no enlightenment outside the mind.

Those who understand these words, will know bliss.

Hui-neng 3

The illusion of ignorance

Good people, in our system of meditation we do not contemplate the mind, nor do we contemplate perfect wisdom. And we do not approve of inactivity.

We do not contemplate the mind, because the individual mind is an illusion; and since it is an illusion, contemplating it would strengthen the illusion. We do not contemplate perfect wisdom, because we are already perfectly wise; all ignorance is illusory. So if we contemplated perfect wisdom, we should create another illusion, the illusion of becoming wise. When we shatter all illusions, perfect wisdom is manifest.

Perfect wisdom has no shape or form. Some people speak of the shape or form of perfect wisdom, as if perfect wisdom could be defined. Yet any attempt to define perfect wisdom merely reveals the ignorance of the person making the attempt.

Good people, in training yourselves to realize perfect wisdom, you should not be disturbed by the faults of others. You should be indifferent as to whether others are good or evil; by making moral judgements on others, you upset yourself. Ignorant people take pleasure in criticizing those around them; and in this way they maintain their ignorance.

Hui-neng 5

Detachment and serenity

Good people, the purpose of meditation is to gain freedom from ignorance, and to be serene in all circumstances, whether those circumstances are good or bad. To meditate is to seek wisdom and serenity within yourself.

Through meditation you detach yourself from all external objects; and this leads to inner serenity. If you are attached to external objects, you are constantly disturbed; but when you are free from attachments, you are at peace. Attachment leads to disturbance because it makes you a slave to the objects of your attachment; when these objects change, you are upset. Those who learn to detach themselves completely from external objects, enjoy complete serenity.

Be vigilant at all times. Attachment constantly reasserts itself. So you must constantly strive for detachment.

Hui-neng 5

Dispelling the clouds of attachment

All things are only figments and manifestations of the mind. Thus good deeds come from good thoughts in the mind; and evil deeds come from evil thoughts in the mind. The mind already possesses perfect wisdom.

The bright azure of the sky and the bright beam of the sun are frequently obscured by clouds; and in their ignorance people may imagine that the brightness of the sky and the sun have dimmed. But as soon as the clouds have passed, it becomes clear that the sky and the sun are as bright as ever.

Good people, evil habits may be compared with the clouds, and perfect wisdom may be compared with the sun. When you attach yourself to external objects, you cloud your mind, and you prevent perfect wisdom from shedding its light.

But happily there are many good and enlightened teachers who can show you the Way – the Way leading to the realization of perfect wisdom. Once you have been shown the Way, then by your own efforts you may follow it, dispelling every kind of illusion.

Good people, remove from your minds all clouds of jealousy, vanity, pride, deceit, falsehood, disdain, snobbery, and arrogance. Listen to those who draw your attention to these clouds; and be constantly on the alert, looking for them yourself. When the clouds of attachment have gone, the light may shine without hindrance.

Hui-neng 6

The paradox of good and evil

Imagine taking a lamp into a place which has been dark for a thousand years; that lamp will instantly pierce the darkness, and dispel it. In the same way a single spark of wisdom can dispel ignorance that has lasted for aeons.

Do not worry about the past; the past is over, and cannot be recovered. Concentrate on the future; in particular, concentrate on the next moment, dispelling all darkness from your mind.

To the ignorant mind good and evil are opposites. To the wise mind there can be no duality, only unity. True unity cannot be polluted by evil, nor can it be cleansed by goodness. Yet one evil thought can spoil the merit accumulated over many lives; and one good thought can expiate the sins of many lives. So watch over the mind, ensuring that only good thoughts pass through it; by this means you will move towards enlightenment, in which there is neither good nor evil.

Hui-neng 6

Reality and religion

Good people, I shall soon be leaving this world. Let me summarize my answers to all the questions which you have asked me.

Nothing external is real; free yourselves from the notion that external objects have reality. Those who believe that external objects are real, are enslaved by this belief. External objects are illusory; they are figments of the mind. Reality is found within the mind; so those who know the mind, know reality.

Living beings are mobile, whereas inanimate objects are stationary. If you train yourself to keep still, ceasing to move at all, you will gain no benefit; on the contrary, you will become no better than an inanimate object. True stillness is stillness within activity; it is inner stillness, that is not disturbed by outer movement.

If you wish to follow the Way, you must exert yourselves, keeping watch constantly over your mind. Dispel every kind of illusory knowledge, which binds you to the wheel of birth and death.

There are many different religions in the world. Be courteous to people of all religions, and strive to please them. Religious doctrines are unimportant; so disputes on doctrinal matters should be shunned.

Hui-neng 10

Perfect wisdom for a moment

Perfect wisdom is all that matters. Through enlightenment you will realize the perfect wisdom within you. To attain enlightenment you must dispel all illusions from your mind. If you sow the seed of reality within your mind, you will reap the fruit of enlightenment.

Do not allow the purity of your mind to be defiled by sensual desires. Sensual desires lead to attachment to external objects. Thus by ridding yourself of desires, you detach yourself from illusions.

If you realize perfect wisdom for a single moment, then the whole truth is known to you. And perfect wisdom can only be realized for a single moment.

Those who think that perfect wisdom can be realized by believing certain doctrines, will never realize perfect wisdom. Those who think that perfect wisdom can be realized by studying external objects, will never realize perfect wisdom. Only those who look within themselves for perfect wisdom, will realize it.

Hui-neng 10

Not this and not that

Good people, take care of yourselves. After I have died, do not weep or grieve, as is customary. Do not accept messages of condolence, and do not wear mourning clothes. Marking death in these ways is contrary to all that I have taught you.

All that I ask is that you know your own mind, and realize perfect wisdom within yourselves. Perfect wisdom is neither stationary nor mobile; it neither becomes nor ceases; it neither comes nor goes; it neither affirms nor denies; it neither stays nor departs.

Remember my words, and repeat them, striving to understand my meaning. When you fully understand my meaning, the illusions within your minds will be shattered. If after my death you continue to carry out my instructions, my death will make no difference to you. But if you are determined to go against my teachings, then my continued presence would confer no benefit.

Enlightened people are serene; and their serenity cannot be disturbed. They practise no virtues. They are self-possessed and dispassionate. They practise no vices. They are calm and silent. They do not see or hear external objects. They are tranquil and incorruptible. Their minds are nowhere.

I have said all that I need to say. Now I shall die.

Hui-neng 10

A nail into the sky

Linji addressed the monks: 'By speaking to you today, I am submitting to your request. If I were to discuss the meaning of Buddhism, I should not open my mouth; and if you knew I were to discuss the meaning of Buddhism, you would not attend. Perhaps there are some brave warriors amongst you, who would like to unfurl their banners.'

A monk asked: 'What is the meaning of Buddhism?' Linji gave a shout. The monk bowed. Linji said: 'This is the kind of monk whom it is worth addressing.'

A monk asked: 'What is the meaning of your teaching?' Linji replied: 'When I put that question to Huang-Po, who was my teacher, he hit me. When I put it again, he hit me a second time. When I put it again, he hit me a third time.' The monk was about to speak. Linji gave a shout, and hit him, saying: 'You do not drive a nail into the sky.'

Linji addressed the monks again: 'I am here to discuss the meaning of Buddhism. Does anyone have any further questions? If so, ask them quickly. But if you open your mouth, you will say nothing about the meaning of Buddhism. This is because the meaning of Buddhism cannot be encapsulated in words. So I shall withdraw.'

                                        Linji 1

Lump of flesh

Linji addressed the monks: 'Look at this lump of flesh which is my body. Inside is a soul which has no status. The face is the gateway for the soul, through which the soul goes out and comes in. If any of you are uncertain of this, just look.' A monk asked: 'Describe this soul that has no status.' Linji ran to the monk, took hold of him, and shouted in his face: 'Speak! Speak!' The monk began to speak. Linji pushed him away, exclaiming: 'Why should I listen to a soul with no status?'

A monk asked: 'What is the meaning of Buddhism?' Linji held up his fly-whisk. The monk gave a shout; and Linji gave a shout. The monk began to speak. Linji ran to the monk, and hit him.

Linji addressed the monks again: 'For the sake of the Way, be prepared to sacrifice the lump of flesh which is your body. When I asked Huang-Po about the meaning of Buddhism, he hit me. When I asked him again, he hit me a second time. When I asked him again, he hit me a third time. I wish I could be hit again now. Are any of you willing to hit me?' A monk stepped forward, and said: 'I am willing to hit you.' Linji picked up a stick, and offered it to the monk. But before the monk could take it, Linji hit him with it.

Linji 3, 5

The mountain and the city

Linji addressed the monks: 'A person is sitting alone on the top of a remote mountain peak; yet this person is not detached from the world. Another person is walking along a city street; yet this person has no desires or attachments. Which of these people is more spiritually advanced? Do not imagine I am talking about others; I am talking about you.'

Linji continued: 'One person is physically on the road, but spiritually has not left home. Another person is spiritually on the road, but physically has not left home. Which of these people is more worthy of respect?' With this question Linji departed.

Linji 7, 8

A burning house

Linji addressed the monks: 'A good teacher draws out that which is within people. Do not be led astray by bad teachers. Follow that which is within you; follow without doubt or hesitation.

'If you fail to make progress, what is the reason? The reason is that you do not have faith in yourself. If you do not have faith in yourself, you will be constantly hurrying to keep up with those around you; you will be swayed this way and that, according to the company you are in. But if you stop rushing and look within, you will be like the Buddha. The Buddha is no different from you.

'Do not delay. If you fail to find truth in this life, you will be reborn a thousand more times, or even ten thousand. You might be reborn from the belly of a donkey or a cow.

'Yes, we are no different from the Buddha. In our activities each day, are we deficient in anything? Each of us can see, hear, smell, taste, feel and think just like the Buddha. If only you could see yourself as the same as the Buddha, then you would be the same as the Buddha.

'The external world is like a burning house; escape from it as quickly as you can. The external world is like a disease which destroys you, whether you are rich or poor, old or young.'

Linji 11

Looking for a lost mind

Linji continued: 'When it is time to dress, put on your clothes. When you wish to go for a walk, go for a walk. When you wish to sit down, sit down. But never for a moment strive to be like the Buddha. Why not? If you strive to be like the Buddha, you will remain in the realm of birth, death and rebirth.

'Time is precious. You eagerly study Zen, and you study the teachings of the Buddha. You cling to words, and learn phrases by heart. You seek out teachers who can guide you. You are constantly planning your spiritual progress. Stop. Look carefully at yourself. A man lost his mind, and went to look for it; only when he stopped looking for it, did he find it.

'Just act normally. Do not act in a special religious manner. There are some monks with shaven heads who cannot tell goodness from evil. Yet they are constantly seeing angels here and devils there; and they declare that they love both sunshine and rain. Many people are taken in by those who act religiously, and give them copious amounts of food. But one day the supporters of religious people will realize that their food has been wasted.'

Linji 11

The distance of the sky from the earth

Linji addressed the monks: 'Go wherever you want in the world; but do not become muddled. The person of true value has nothing to do. So do not try to act in a special religious manner; just act normally. Do not look for anything, not even the Buddha; after all, "Buddha" is just a word.

'Why is everyone rushing around? People are looking for the Way in all directions. You have come here in search of the Way. Once you know the Way, all will be well; but until then you will be reborn again and again.

'What is this thing called the Way? The Way is the truth of the mind. The truth of the mind has no fixed form; it is everywhere, and is right before your eyes. But since people lack faith in themselves, they cling to words, and learn phrases by heart. They look for the Way in books. But they are as far away from the Way as the sky is from the earth.

'When I speak about the Way, what am I speaking about? I speak about the Way of the mind. The Way is thus found in wise people and foolish people, good people and bad people, religious people and irreligious people. In fact, when you understand the Way, you realize that people are neither wise nor foolish, neither good nor bad, neither religious nor irreligious.

'When people ask me about the Way, I see through them. I don't look at how they appear, but how they are.'

Linji 12

Putting on a garment

Linji addressed his monks: 'If you depend on nothing, then you belong to the realm of enlightenment. If you know you depend on nothing, then you will always belong to the realm of enlightenment. But if you keep making distinctions, such as that between wise people and ordinary people, you do not belong to the realm of enlightenment.

'Do you want to be free to be born or die as you choose? Do you want to be born with the ease of putting on a garment, and die with the ease of taking off a garment? If so, you need to understand that you, in your reality, have no form, no origin, no beginning, no permanent home – and yet are alive.

'Do not make some dream or fantasy your companion on the Way. A dream embodies a desire for permanence; and sooner or later you must recognize that nothing is permanent.

'While you are in this world, where do you look for salvation? Do you think eating will save you? Do you think patching up your clothes will save you? Do you think finding the right teacher will save you? You will not find salvation in any object or living being.

'Time is precious. Soon your body will disintegrate into the four elements with which it is made.'

Linji 15

The four elements

Linji addressed the monks: 'If your mind is beset by doubt, then the element of earth is obstructing it. If your mind is beset by desire, then the element of water is drowning it. If your mind is beset by anger, then the element of fire is burning it. If your mind is beset by delight, then the element of air is tossing it about.

'If you understand how the four elements affect the mind, then you will not be subject to your environment, but will be able to use your environment for your own purposes. You will be able to move across the earth at will, going east, south, north and west as you wish. You will be able to walk on water as if it were earth. How will you be able to do this? You will be able to do this because you will know that the elements are figments of the mind.

'Listen to the Way which lies within your soul, and not to the elements with which it is made.

'Do you want to be wise? Wise is just a word. There are people who go up a high mountain in search of wisdom. They are wrong! Wisdom is not to be found on a high mountain. Wisdom is here. Wisdom is to be found in carrying out your daily activities. Wisdom is in our routine, which never changes. Wisdom is in the light which shines in your mind.'

Linji 16

Good crimes

Linji addressed the monks: 'There are five things that are commonly regarded as unforgivable crimes. They are killing your father, injuring your mother, desecrating the Buddha's body, disrupting the monastic community, and burning the sacred texts.'

The monk asked: 'What is meant by the father?' Linji replied: 'Ignorance is the father. When your mind is like an echo responding to emptiness, when it is totally inactive, this is killing the father.'

The monk asked: 'What is meant by the mother?' Linji replied: 'Greed is the mother. When your mind does not respond to external objects with desire, and hence has no attachments, this is injuring the mother.'

The monk asked: 'What is meant by the Buddha's body?' Linji replied: 'Distinguishing between one object and another is the Buddha's body. When your mind regards all things as one, this is desecrating the Buddha's body.'

The monk asked: 'What is meant by the monastic community?' Linji replied: 'Worldly entanglements are the monastic community. When your mind is free of all entanglements, this is disrupting the monastic community.

The monk asked: 'What is meant by the sacred texts?' Linji replied: 'Distinctions between wisdom and folly are the sacred texts. When your mind regards all people as one, this is burning the sacred texts.'

Linji 23

Leaning on the sunshine

Linji continued: 'Moment by moment your mind confronts a shaking fist or a pointing finger, and you imagine these images to be real. You blunder about in the realm of the senses. And you excuse yourself, exclaiming that you are just a common mortal.

'You idiot! You put on the skin of a lion, and then yap like a jackal. You do not trust what you possess within yourself, and look outside yourself. You fill your mind with the idle words and phrases of ancient sages. You cling to shadows, and lean on the sunshine, instead of standing on your own. You clutch at passing grains of dust.

'Do not take seriously my words and phrases; no utterance of mine has foundations – my words and phrases are painted on the sky. Do not think the Buddha is your ultimate goal; think of him as the hole in a latrine – you cannot possess the Buddha. Do not try to understand the sacred texts; simply try to understand. Even if you could understand every sacred text in existence, you would not be as good as the monk who does nothing.

'You go around puffing up your chest, and declaring that you understand Zen, that you understand the Way. The principles of the Way cannot be understood with the mind; so you cannot claim with your mind that you understand it.'

Linji 23

A hair absorbing an ocean

Linji went with another monk, called Pu-hua, to eat at the home of a lay disciple. Linji said: 'One hair absorbs a vast ocean; one seed holds a high mountain. Are these things revelations of a higher power; or are they part of the natural order?' Pu-hua kicked over the tray on which his food had been served. Linji exclaimed: 'Too rude!' Pu-hua said: 'How dare you talk to me about what is rude and what is polite!'

The following day Linji and Pu-hua went to eat at the home of another lay disciple. Linji said: 'Is the food today better than the food yesterday?' As before, Pu-hua kicked over the tray on which his food had been served. Linji exclaimed: 'Still too coarse!' Pu-hua said: 'In the Way of the Buddha there is no distinction between what is rude and what is polite.' Linji stuck out his tongue.

Linji 26

Braying like a donkey

Linji was sitting with two elderly monks around a fire. One of the monks remarked: 'That monk Pu-hua goes around the streets of the town each day behaving like an idiot. I cannot decide whether he is wise or mad.' At that moment Pu-hua appeared. Linji asked him: 'Are you wise or mad?' Pu-hua replied: 'You tell me whether I am wise or mad.' Linji gave a shout. Pu-hua pointed at one of the elderly monks, and said: 'You are a new bride.' Then he pointed at the other elderly monk, and said: 'You are an old grandmother.' Finally he pointed to Linji, and said: 'You are a brat – but you see things.' Linji exclaimed: 'You are a thief.' Pu-hua cried: 'Thief! Thief!' Then he ran away.

The next day Pu-hua sat amongst the other monks, eating raw vegetables. Linji saw him, and said: 'You are a donkey.' Pu-hua brayed like a donkey, and cried: 'Thief! Thief!' Then he ran away.

Linji 27, 28

Asking the questions

Joshu addressed the monks: 'The true Way is not difficult. Those who follow the Way, need only reject choice and attachment. A single word may stimulate the urge to choose, or may evoke the urge towards attachment; or a single word may lead to enlightenment. Although I am old, I do not have enlightenment. Do you understand this, or not?'

A monk asked: 'If you do not have enlightenment, what do you understand?' Joshu replied: 'I do not understand that, either.' The monk said: 'If you do not understand, how can you say that you do not have enlightenment?' Joshu said: 'Asking the question is good enough. Now bow to me, and retire.'

Setcho 2

The world as a grain of rice

Seppo addressed the monks: 'If I were to pick up the world and place it on the palm of my hand, it would seem like a grain of rice. If I were to throw it at your face, you would not see it; you would have to beat the drum, summoning every monk to search for it.'

Ummon addressed the monks: 'Ignore the first fourteen days of the month. Tell me about the last fourteen days. Say a good word about them.' No one replied. So Ummon supplied his own answer: 'Every day is a good day.'

Suigan at the end of the summer addressed the monks: 'During the summer I have talked a great deal to you. Now, look! Have I any eyebrows?' One monk said: 'A man who commits theft, has a guilty conscience.' Another monk said: 'They have grown.' Ummon said: 'Wonderful!'

A monk asked Joshu: 'What is Joshu?' Joshu replied: 'The east gate, the west gate, the north gate, and the south gate.'

Setcho 5, 6, 8, 9

Snow in a silver bowl

Obaku addressed the monks: 'You all drink beer. If you continue to study Zen as you drink beer, you will never finish it.
Do you know that in this entire country there is not a single
Zen teacher.' A monk said: 'But there are many who give
lectures and teach monks. What about that?' Obaku replied:
'I do not say there is no Zen; I merely say there is no Zen
teacher.'

A monk asked Tozan: 'What is enlightenment?' Tozan
replied: 'A bag of flax.'

A monk asked Haryo: 'What is Zen?' Haryo replied: 'Snow
in a silver bowl.'

A monk asked Ummon: 'What is the Buddha's teaching?'
Ummon replied: 'Unity.'

A monk asked Ummon: 'What does it signify when the
mind is empty of thought?' Ummon replied: 'Unity – which
cannot be learnt.'

A monk asked Kyorin: 'What is the meaning of the
Buddha's Way coming from India to China?' Kyorin replied:
'Sitting long, and getting tired.'

Setcho 11, 12, 13, 14, 15, 17

The sound of one hand clapping

The emperor asked Kokushi: 'When you are a hundred years old, what shall I do for you?' Kokushi answered: 'Make a perfect pagoda for an old monk.' The emperor asked: 'What style should it be?' Kokushi remained silent for a while. Then he asked the emperor: 'Do you understand?' The emperor said: 'No, I do not.' Kokushi said: 'I have a disciple called Tangen. He will succeed me as a teacher. Ask him.'

Kokushi died before reaching the age of a hundred. Yet the emperor still wanted to build a pagoda in his honour. So he sent for Tangen, and asked him in what style he should make the pagoda. Tangen said: 'To the south and the north, make it from the sound of one hand clapping. In between use wooden beams as large as mountains. Plant beside it a tree that gives no shade. When it is complete, say: "All is complete."'

Setcho 18

In and out of the water

A monk asked Chimon: 'What is the lotus when it is in the water?' Chimon replied: 'The lotus flower.' Then the monk asked: 'What is the lotus when it is out of the water?' Chimon replied: 'Lotus leaves.'

Hofuku and Chokei went out for a walk in the fields. Hofuku pointed with his finger, and said: 'This is marvellous.' Chokei said: 'You are right. But alas.' A monk related this exchange to Kyosei, who said: 'If Chokei had not spoken, the fields would have been littered with skulls.'

A monk came to Isan in his hut. Isan said: 'You old female buffalo, you have come.' The monk said: 'Tomorrow there is a great festival in the town. Will you be going?' Isan lay down, and stretched himself out. The monk went away.

A Zen teacher held out his staff, and said to his disciples: 'When in olden times people attained a state of enlightenment, why did they not remain there?' No one answered. So the teacher gave his own reply: 'Because enlightenment is useless in this world.' He paused, and added: 'After all, what can you do with it?' Then he gave a further reply: 'Taking no notice of others an enlightened man puts his staff on his shoulder, goes straight ahead, and journeys into the deepest recesses of a hundred thousand mountains.'

Setcho 21, 23, 24, 25

Growing radishes

A monk asked Hyakujo: 'What is the most wonderful thing
in the world?' Hyakujo replied: 'I am the most wonderful
thing in the world.' The monk bowed. Hyakujo struck him.

A monk asked Ummon: 'Why do the leaves wither and
fall?' Ummon replied: 'You embody the golden breeze of au-
tumn that makes them fall.'

Hyakujo came to see Nansen, and asked: 'Is there any aspect of the Way that has not been preached to the common
people?' 'Yes, there is,' Nansen replied. Hyakujo asked: 'What
aspect of the Way has not been preached to the common
people?' Nansen replied: 'The Way is not mind; it is not the
Buddha; it is nothing.' Then Nansen added: 'I have not
preached that. Have you?' Hyakujo replied: 'I have very little
wisdom. How can I tell whether I have preached that?'
Nansen said: 'I do not understand you.' Hyakujo said: 'I have
talked enough.'

A monk asked Daizui: 'When the universe is destroyed,
will truth perish or not?' Daizui replied: 'The truth about the
universe will perish with the universe.'

A monk asked Joshu: 'I have heard that you are a disciple
of Nansen. Is that true.' Joshu replied: 'If you want to grow
radishes, you must find the right soil.'

Setcho 26, 27, 28, 29, 30

A circle in the air

A monk came to Shokei, carrying a bell and a staff. He walked around Shokei's seat three times, ringing the bell; then he stuck his staff in the ground. Shokei exclaimed: 'Good!' Then the monk went to Nansen. He walked around Nansen's seat three times, ringing the bell; then he stuck his staff in the ground. Nansen exclaimed: 'Bad!' The monk said to Nansen: 'I have shown my respects to both Shokei and you. He indicated his approval, whereas you have indicated your disapproval. Why?' Nansen replied: 'You are blown from one teacher to another by the wind. That will lead to destruction.'

A monk asked Linji: 'What is the essence of Buddhism?' Linji rose from his seat, slapped the monk, and pushed him away. The monk stood still. Linji said: 'Why do you not bow?' The monk bowed low; and at that moment he was enlightened.

A monk came to see Shifuku. After a while Shifuku drew a circle in the air with his forefinger. The monk asked: 'Why do you draw a circle?' Shifuku replied: 'You only have one eye.'

Setcho 31, 32, 33

Threes and threes

A Zen teacher called Bunki arrived at the monastery led by
Manjusri. After welcoming Bunki, Manjusri asked: 'From
where have you come?' Bunki replied: 'I have come from the
south.' Manjusri asked: 'How is Buddhism faring in the
south?' Bunki replied: 'The monks today are less devout
than the monks of old.' Manjusri asked: 'Are there many or
few monks in the south?' Bunki replied: 'There are about
three hundred monks in one place, and five hundred monks
in another.'

Then Bunki asked: 'How is Buddhism faring in the north?'
Manjusri replied: 'There are both worldly monks and holy
monks; and they are living together. Dragons and snakes are
mingled.' Bunki asked: 'Are there many or few monks in the
north?' Manjusri: 'In one place there are threes and threes;
and in another place there are threes and threes.'

Setcho 35

Whales and frogs

On a day in spring Chosha went for a walk. When he returned, a monk asked: 'Where have you been walking?' Chosha replied: 'I have been walking in the hills.' The monk asked: 'What route did you take?' Chosha replied: 'First I followed the fragrant grasses; and then I went after the scented blossoms.' The monk said: 'Are you not taking much pleasure in the spring?' Chosha replied: 'Better the positive serenity of fresh flowers, than the negative serenity of falling leaves.'

Fuketsu addressed the monks: 'Consider a seal on molten wax. If the seal is removed, the impression appears; but if the seal is not removed, the impression does not appear.' A monk said: 'I ask you not to press down the seal.' Fuketsu replied: 'For a long time I have been hunting whales in the great ocean. I feel irritated at finding a frog tumbling about in muddy water.' The monk said nothing. Fuketsu gave a shout, and said: 'Why do you not continue with what you were saying?' The monk still remained silent. Fuketsu lifted his staff, as if he were about to strike the monk. The monk began to speak. Fuketsu struck him.

Setcho 36, 38

A fence around a flower garden

A monk asked Ummon: 'How should I understand the body of the Buddha?' Ummon replied: 'Think of the body of the Buddha as a fence around a flower garden.'

A monk said to Nansen: 'I have heard people say that happiness and misery are one and the same. Is not this absurd?' Nansen pointed to a flower, and asked: 'Do you see just a flower, or do you see truth?'

A monk asked Tosu: 'Is it possible for a person to enter nirvana, and then return?' Tosu replied: 'Do not ask questions when you are still in darkness; you are like a thief at night. Wait until you have attained enlightenment; then you will understand.'

A monk said to Tozan: 'In winter we are cold, and in the summer we are hot. How can we avoid cold and heat?' Tozan said: 'Why do you not go where there is neither cold nor heat?' The monk asked: 'Where is that place where there is neither cold nor heat?' Tozan replied: 'When it is cold, let the coldness kill you. When it is hot, let the heat kill you.'

Setcho 39, 40, 41, 43

Beating the drum

Kasan addressed the monks: 'When you are distant from the truth, you need to listen. When you are close to the truth, you no longer need to listen. Then you transcend both distance and closeness; this is the moment of enlightenment.'

A monk asked: 'What is meant by enlightenment?' Kasan answered: 'Beating the drum.'

The monk asked: 'What is the genuine teaching of the Buddha?' Kasan answered: 'Beating the drum.'

The monk asked: 'What is the mind of the Buddha?' Kasan answered: 'Beating the drum.'

The monk asked: 'What is the non-mind of the Buddha?' Kasan answered: 'Beating the drum.'

The monk asked: 'When an enlightened person appears, by what means should we greet that person?' Kasan answered: 'Beating the drum.'

Setcho 44

A carp out of a net

A monk said to Joshu: 'All spiritual teaching boils down to oneness. What does oneness boil down to?' Joshu replied: 'Recently I made a shirt out of hemp. It felt rough.'

It was raining. Kyosei asked his monks: 'What is the noise outside?' A monk replied: 'It is the voice of raindrops.' Kyosei said: 'You are deluded.' The monk asked: 'Are you also deluded?' Kyosei replied: 'I was near it, but I am not deluded.' The monk asked: 'What do you mean by saying that you were near it, but are not deluded?' Kyosei replied: 'I understand delusion, so I am near it; I transcend delusion, so I am not deluded.'

A monk said to Seppo: 'When a golden carp is caught in a net, and then taken out of the net, what does it feed on?' Seppo replied: 'When you are out of the net, I shall tell you.' The monk asked: 'Why can you not tell me now?' Seppo replied: 'I have many matters pressing for my attention.'

Setcho 45, 46, 49

The last word

Seppo went to live as a hermit in the southern mountains. In due course two monks came to his hermitage to pay their respects. He came out to meet them, and asked: 'What is this?' The monks also said: 'What is this?' Seppo lowered his head, and went back inside.

Later the two monks went to Ganto. He came out to meet them, and asked: 'Where are you from?' The monks answered: 'We come from the mountains in the south.' Ganto asked: 'Have you been to see Seppo?' The monks replied that they had. Ganto asked: 'What did he say to you?' The monks described their encounter with Seppo. Ganto then said: 'I regret that, when I was with him, I did not tell him the last word. If I had done so, you would not have dared to insult him.'

Some months passed. The two monks then returned to Ganto, and asked him to teach them. Ganto said: 'Why did you not ask earlier?' The monks replied: 'We did not understand how much we needed teaching.' Ganto said: 'Seppo became enlightened in the same way that I did; but he does not behave as I do. If you want to know the last word, I shall tell you. It is, "This! This!"'

Setcho 51

The stone bridge

A monk came to Joshu, and said: 'Your stone bridge is famous. Yet I come here, and only find stepping-stones.' Joshu replied: 'You see only stepping-stones; but that does not mean there is no stone bridge.' The monk asked: What is the stone bridge?' Joshu replied: 'Any living creature, even horses and donkeys, can cross the river of birth and death.'

Baso went for a walk with a monk. They saw a wild duck fly past. Baso asked: 'What is that?' The monk replied: 'It is a wild duck.' Baso asked: 'Where is it?' The monk replied: 'It has flown away.' Baso pinched the monk's nose hard; and the monk cried out in pain. Baso exclaimed: 'There! How can it fly away?'

A monk came to Ummon, and said: 'I have come from the teacher Saizan.' Ummon asked: 'What words has Saizan offered lately?' The monk stretched out his hands. Ummon struck him. The monk said: 'I was about to speak.' Ummon stretched out his own hands. The monk was silent. Ummon struck him again.

Setcho 52, 53, 54

Dogo heard that a certain person in the locality had died, and went to visit the person's family; he was accompanied by a disciple, called Zengen. When they arrived, Zengen touched the coffin, and asked Dogo: 'Is this life, or is this death?' Dogo replied: 'I shall not tell you whether it is life or death.' Zengen asked: 'Why will you not tell me?' Dogo said again: 'I shall not tell you whether it is life or death.'

On their way home, Zengen said: 'If you do not tell me whether it is life or death, I shall hit you.' Dogo said: 'You may hit me, if you wish. But I shall not tell you whether it is life or death.' Zengen hit him.

Some years later Dogo died. Zengen went to Sekiso, and told him the story of visiting the bereaved family. And then Zengen asked: 'Is it life, or is it death.' Sekiso replied: 'I shall not tell you whether it is life or death.' On hearing these words again, Zengen attained enlightenment.

Soon afterwards Sekiso saw Zengen wandering around, as if he were searching for something. Sekiso asked: 'What are you searching for?' Zengen replied: 'I am searching for the spiritual remains of my dead teacher.' Sekiso said: 'The dead teacher's spiritual remains pervade the entire universe. So why do you search?' Zengen replied: 'It is a way of expressing gratitude.'

Setcho 55

Something said

A monk said to Joshu: 'It is said that the Way is not difficult; it merely requires the rejection of choice and attachment. What are non-choice and non-attachment?' Joshu replied: 'I am famed for my holiness throughout the earth.' The monk said: 'Clearly you have chosen to be holy, and you are attached to fame.' Joshu said: 'So you already understand non-choice and non-attachment.'

Some years later another monk said to Joshu: 'You often say that the Way is not difficult; it merely requires the rejection of choice and attachment. Is not your repetition of this statement a sign of attachment?' Joshu replied: 'I cannot justify the statement.'

A monk said to Joshu: 'It is said that the Way is not difficult; it merely requires the rejection of choice and attachment. Yet it seems to me that wanting to help others is a matter of choice, and a sign of attachment. So how can I help others without deviating from the Way.' Joshu asked: 'Do people say anything more about the Way?' The monk replied: 'I only know this much.' Joshu said: 'Then you already understand the answer.'

Setcho 57, 58, 59

A staff into a dragon

Ummon held out his staff, and said to the monks: 'This staff has transformed itself into a dragon, and swallowed up the universe. Where are the mountains and the rivers? Where is the world itself?'

Fuketsu said to the monks: 'If the mind stirs, the whole universe comes into being. If the mind becomes still, the whole universe ceases to exist.'

Ummon said to the monks: 'Within the entire universe there is a single treasure. It is hidden in a great mountain. With your mind as your lantern, you can enter the mountain and find it.'

Nansen was going with two monks to visit another Zen teacher. When they had walked half the distance, Nansen drew a circle on the ground. And he said to the monks: 'If you can say a word, I shall go with you.' One monk sat down in the middle of the circle. The other monk bowed from the waist, as a woman does. Nansen said: 'Then I shall not go.' One of the monks said: 'You rascal!'

Setcho 60, 61, 62, 69

Closed mouth and lips

Hyakujo said to a monk: 'If you kept your mouth and lips closed, how would you speak the truth?' The monk said: 'I should ask you to speak it.' Hyakujo said: 'I could speak it. But if I did so, I should have no successors.'

Hyakujo said to a second monk: 'If you kept your mouth and lips closed, how would you speak the truth?' The monk said: 'I should ask you to remain silent.' Hyakujo said: 'In the state of total tranquillity, where nothing stirs, I shall watch over you.'

Hyakujo said to a third monk: 'If you kept your mouth and lips closed, how would you speak the truth?' The monk said: 'Have you asked that question with your mouth and lips closed?' Hyakujo said: 'I shall have no successors.'

Setcho 70, 71, 72

Flowers and leaves

A monk said to Tosu: 'It is said that every voice is the Buddha's voice. Is that true?' Tosu replied: 'Yes, it is true.' The monk said: 'In that case, do not let me hear you breaking wind.' Tosu struck him with a stick.

Then the monk said to Tosu: 'It is said that rough words and smooth words may be used to preach the Way. Is that true?' Tosu replied: 'Yes, it is true.' The monk said: 'In that case, may I call you a donkey?' Tosu struck him with a stick.

A monk said to Tairyu: 'The human body eventually decomposes. Is there an indestructible body?' Tairyu replied: 'Every year the flowers cover the hillside like a carpet; and leaves come out on the trees, giving shade to the valleys.'

Ummon said to the monks: 'You each have your own light. But if you try to see your light, you will be surrounded by darkness. Where is everybody's light?' No one answered. He supplied an answer himself: 'You can find the halls and the gates of this monastery. Your light is even closer than they are.' Then he added: 'Nothing is better than nothing.'

Ummon addressed the monks: 'Medicine cures sickness, and sickness defeats medicine. All the earth is medicine. Where are you?'

Setcho 79, 82, 86, 87

The dead fox

Hyakujo was delivering a series of lectures. At the start of each lecture an old man slipped into the lecture hall, unseen by the monks; and at the end he slipped out. But after one lecture he remained behind. Hyakujo asked: 'Who are you?'

The old man replied: 'I am not now a human being. But I was once a Zen teacher, living on this mountain. One of my disciples asked me whether an enlightened person is subject to the law of causation. I replied that an enlightened person is not subject to the law of causation. For giving such a literal and absolute answer, I was reborn as a fox; and I have been reborn as a fox five hundred times. Will you save me from this condition? Please tell me whether an enlightened person is subject to the law of causation.'

Hyakujo replied: 'An enlightened person is at one with the law of causation.' At these words the old man exclaimed: 'I am saved!' He bowed low to Hyakujo, and said: 'I am no longer a fox. I must go and leave my body in my cave on the other side of the mountain.' Then he ran off.

The following day Hyakujo ordered the monastery cook to prepare a funeral meal. The cook said: 'No one has died in the monastery.' Hyakujo insisted. As the meal was being prepared, Hyakujo led a group of monks to a cave on the other side of the mountain. There they found a dead fox; and Hyakujo ordered his monks to cremate it. Then they returned to the monastery, and ate the funeral meal.

Mumon 2

The finger of enlightenment

Gutei raised his finger whenever he was asked a question. A boy, who was a servant at the monastery, began to imitate this mannerism.

When Gutei saw that the boy was imitating him, he seized the boy, and cut off his finger. The boy cried, and ran away. Gutei called out to the boy. The boy stopped, and turned towards Gutei. At that moment Gutei raised up his own finger. At that moment the boy was enlightened.

Many years later, when Gutei was dying, he summoned the monks, and said to them: 'My own teacher taught me the value of the finger as a means of enlightenment. I have used it many times, and I could not exhaust it.' With these words he died.

Mumon 3

Hanging by teeth

Someone asked Kyogen to define Zen. Kyogen replied: 'Zen is like a man who falls off a cliff. A tree is growing just below the edge of the cliff. The man saves himself by hanging on to a branch with his teeth. His feet are dangling in the air; and his hands have been wounded, so he cannot use them to hold on to the tree.

'Then someone comes, looks over the cliff, and asks: "Why did the Buddha's teaching come from India to China?" If the man does not answer, the newcomer will not lift him up. If he does answer, he will fall to the bottom of the cliff, and die. What should he do?'

Mumon 5

Washing the bowl

A young man came to Joshu and said: 'I have just entered the monastery. Please teach me.' Joshu asked: 'Have you eaten the rice porridge that was served to you?' The monk replied: 'I have.' Joshu said: 'Then you had better wash your bowl.' At that moment the monk was enlightened.

The monk then went to a quiet place, and meditated. Some time later Joshu came to find him, and asked: 'Are you present? Are you present?' The monk raised his fist. Joshu said: 'The water is too shallow to anchor here.' With those words he left.

A few days later Joshu again went to visit the monk, and again asked: 'Are you present? Are you present?' The monk again raised his fist. Joshu said: 'Free to give, free to take, free to kill, free to save.' Then he bowed to the monk.

Mumon 7, 11

Cutting a cat

Joshu went away, leaving Nansen behind. Nansen saw two
groups of monks fighting over a cat. Nansen seized the cat
himself, held it up, and said: 'If any of you can give an answer, you can save the cat. If not, I shall kill it.' No one gave
an answer; so Nansen cut the cat in two. That evening Joshu
returned home; and Nansen told him about the incident.
Joshu removed his sandals, placed them on his head, and
walked out. Nansen called out: 'If you had been there, you
would have saved the cat.'

Some days later Joshu asked Nansen: 'What is the Way?'
Nansen said: 'Everyday life is the Way.' Joshu asked: 'Can it
be studied?' Nansen replied: 'If you try to study it, you will
be far away from it.' Joshu persisted: 'How can I know the
Way, if I do not study it?' Nansen replied: 'The Way is not a
matter of knowing or not knowing. Knowing is confusion;
not knowing is delusion. When you have truly reached the
Way, you will be in no doubt; you will find the Way as vast
and boundless as the sky. You cannot call the Way either good
or bad.' With these words Joshu attained enlightenment.

Mumon 14, 19

Blowing out a candle

A monk called Tokusan went to see Ryutan. Tokusan arrived in the early evening, and asked many questions. Eventually Ryutan said: 'It is now late into the night. You should retire.' Tokusan bowed, and walked towards the entrance. He paused, and said: 'It is very dark outside.' Ryutan lit a candle, and offered it to him. But as Tokusan was about to take it, Ryutan blew it out. At that moment Tokusan was enlightened. Ryutan asked: 'What has happened?' Tokusan replied: 'From now on I shall not question my teacher.'

The next day Ryutan addressed the monks: 'I see among you a monk, whose teeth are like swords, and whose mouth is like a bowl full of blood. If you were to hit him with a stick, he would not even turn his head to look at you. Some day he will climb the highest mountain, and there he will teach the Way.'

Tokusan rose, and in front of the monks he burned the copies of the sacred texts which he possessed. Then he said: 'The teachings in the sacred texts are very profound. But compared with enlightenment, they are like a single hair in comparison with the sky; they are like a drop of water in comparison with a great ocean.' With these words he left the monastery.

Mumon 28

The way to a temple

A wandering monk asked an old woman the way to a partic-ular temple, where worshippers were said to acquire wisdom. The old woman replied: 'Go straight ahead.' As the monk continued, he overheard the old woman say under her breath: 'Just another dull, respectable monk.'

Some time later the monk related the old woman's remark to Joshu. 'Wait, and I shall investigate this old woman,' said Joshu. The next day Joshu went to the old woman, and asked the way to the temple. She gave the same reply, and made the same remark under her breath. Joshu returned, and said: 'I have investigated that old woman.'

Mumon 31

In two places

Goso related the story of Seijo: 'When she was a baby, Seijo was betrothed to her cousin Ochu. As she grew up, she became very beautiful; and her father wanted to secure a more prestigious match for her. In the meantime she and Ochu had fallen in love. Ochu was heartbroken at not being able to marry Seijo; so he left home, and went up the Yangtze river by boat. At midnight he heard someone running along the bank, and calling his name; it was Seijo. They sailed together to a distant place, here they had two children.

'Five years passed, and they became homesick, yearning to see their parents again. So they climbed into their boat with their two children, and returned home. When they arrived, Ochu left Seijo and the two children in the boat, while he went to her father, to apologize for having taken his daughter away. But the father replied that Seijo had been so upset at Ochu's departure, she had collapsed in a coma; and she had been lying unconscious in bed for the past five years.'

Goso concluded: 'So Seijo was in two places. But where was her soul?'

Mumon 35

A buffalo passing the window

Goso said: 'When you meet a Zen teacher on the road, you cannot greet him with words; but nor can you remain silent before him. So what should you do?'

A monk asked Joshu: 'Why was the Buddha's teaching brought to China?' Joshu replied: 'The oak tree in the garden.'

Goso said: 'A buffalo passes by the window. His head, horns, and four legs go past. But why does the tail not pass also? Remember, the tail is the place from which he controls himself.'

A monk said to Ummon: 'The brilliance of the Buddha silently illuminates the whole universe.' But before he could finish the sentence, Ummon said: 'You are reciting someone else's words.' The monk said: 'Yes, I am.' Ummon said: 'You have left the path.'

Mumon 36, 37, 38, 39

Kicking the vase

Hyakujo wished to open a new monastery; and so he decided to appoint one of the monks in his present monastery to take charge of it. He summoned the monks, and said: 'The person who gives the best answer to a question, will be appointed head of the new monastery.'

Hyakujo took a vase, and filled it with water; then he placed it on the ground. He asked the monks: 'You may not call this a vase. What do you call it?' One monk, who was very senior, said: 'You may not call it a wooden shoe.' Another monk, who was the monastery cook, tipped over the vase with his foot, and walked away.

Hyakujo smiled, and said: 'The senior monk loses.' The monastery cook took charge of the new monastery.

Mumon 40

The severed arm

A monk cut off his arm, and showed the severed arm to Bodhidharma, saying: 'My mind is not peaceful. Pacify my mind.' Bodhidharma said: 'If you bring me that mind, I shall pacify it for you.' The monk said: 'I have searched for my mind, but I cannot take hold of it.' Bodhidharma said: 'Then your mind is already pacified.'

Shuzan held his staff of office before the monks, and said: 'If you call this a staff, you oppose its reality. But if you do not call it a staff, you oppose the fact. So what do you call it?'

Basho said to the monks: 'If you have a staff, I shall give you a staff. But if you have no staff, I shall take it from you.'

Hoen said: 'The two greatest Zen teachers are servants of one another. Who is the greatest servant?'

Sekiso asked: 'How can you proceed further from the top of a pole?' Another teacher said: 'If you sit at the top of a tall pole, you have started on the Way; but you have not gone far. Proceed further, and go in all directions.'

Mumon 41, 43, 44, 45, 46

Three barriers

Tosutu said: 'There are three barriers through which you have to pass.

'The first is profundity. You must delve deeply into your own nature. Tell me: where at this moment is your true nature?

'The second is freedom. When you realize your true nature, you will be able to break free from life and death. Tell me: when you shut your eyes at death, and become a corpse, how can you be free from life and death?

'The third is knowledge. When you are free from life and death, you will be able to know where you are. Tell me: as the four elements of your body separate after death, where will you be?'

Mumon 47

BIBLIOGRAPHY

There are a number of translations of the works represented in this volume. These are the most accessible.

Conze, Edward (tr.), *Perfect Wisdom: The Short Prajnaparamita Texts* (London, Luzac & Co., 1973).

Evans-Wentz, W. Y. (tr.), *Tibetan Yoga* (London and New York, Oxford University Press, 1967).

Kaviratna, Harischandra, (tr.), *Dhammapada* (Pasadena, Theosophical University Press, 1980).

Lhalungpa, Lobsang P., (tr.), *The Life of Milarepa* (New York, E. P. Dutton, 1977).

Mascaro, Juan (tr.), *Dhammapada* (London, Penguin Books, 1973).

Goddard, Dwight, (ed.), *A Buddhist Bible* (Boston, Beacon Press, 1994).

Ling, Trevor, (ed.), *The Buddha's Philosophy of Man: Early Indian Buddhist Dialogues* (London, J. M. Dent & Sons, 1981).

Maurice, David, *The Lion's Roar: An Anthology from the Pali Canon* (London, Rider & Co., 1962).

Mumon and Setcho, *Two Zen Classics*, tr. K. Sekeida (New York, Weatherhill, 1977).

Price, A. F. and Mou-lam, Wong (tr.), *The Diamond Sutra & The Sutra of Hui-neng* (Boston, Shambhala Publications, 1990).

S(h)antideva, *The Bodhicaryavatara*, tr. Kate Crosby and Andrew Skilton (Oxford and New York, Oxford Universtity Press, 1995).

Watson, Burton (tr.), *The Lotus Sutra* (New York, Columbia University Press, 1993).

Watson, Burton (tr.), *The Zen Teachings of Master Lin-chi* (Boston, Shambhala Publications, 1993).

The illustrations in this volume have been taken from Grunwedel, A., *Buddhist Art in India* (London, Bernard Quaritch, 1901).

INDEX OF WRITERS

Works are listed where author unknown.